Entertainment WEEKLY

The 100 Greatest Stars of All Time

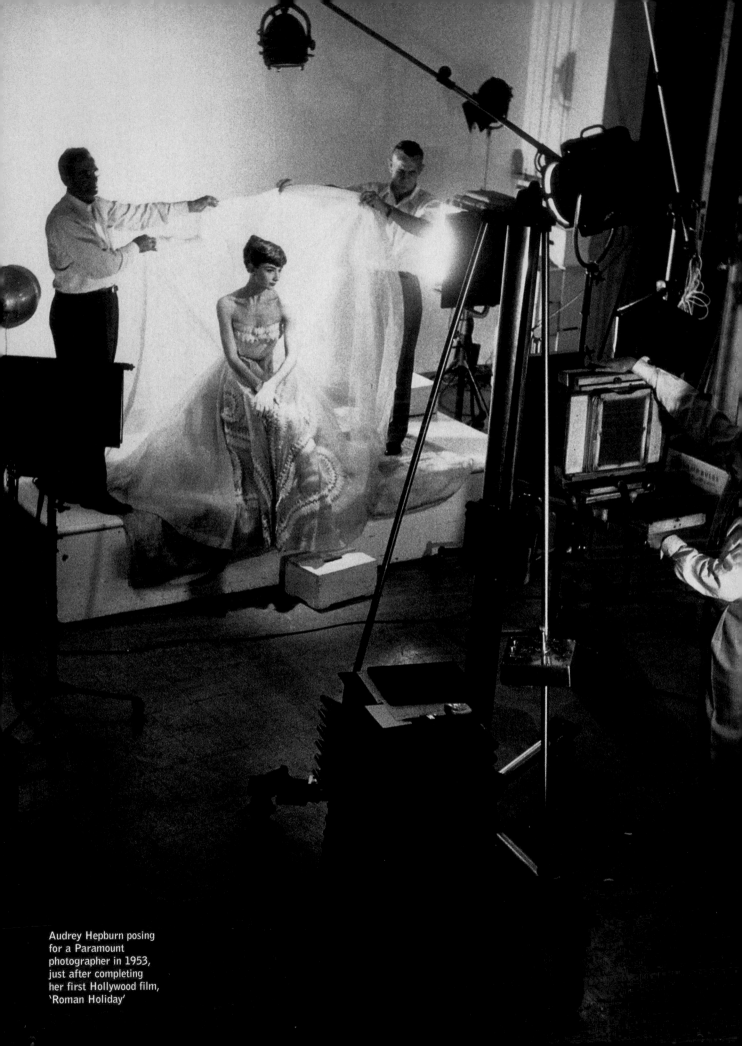

Audrey Hepburn posing for a Paramount photographer in 1953, just after completing her first Hollywood film, 'Roman Holiday'

Contents

Photograph by Bob Willoughby / MPTV

Alison Gwinn | EDITOR   John Korpics | DESIGN DIRECTOR
Ty Burr | SENIOR WRITER   Sarah Rozen | PHOTO EDITOR

Jill Laurinaitis | ASSOCIATE EDITOR

Howard Gutner | REPORTER

Joshua Liberson | DESIGN ASSOCIATE

Ben Spier (chief), Steven Pearl (deputy) | COPY EDITORS

ADDITIONAL STAFF

Martha Babcock, Kristi Huelsing, Tiarra Mukherjee,
Cheo Tyehimba (reporting); Guna Dickson, Maggie Robbins,
Joel Vanliew (copy editing); Eileen O'Sullivan (edit production)

TIME INC. HOME ENTERTAINMENT

David Gitow | MANAGING DIRECTOR

David Arfine | DIRECTOR, CONTINUITIES AND SINGLE SALES

Michael Barrett | DIRECTOR, CONTINUITIES AND RETENTION

Alicia Longobardo | DIRECTOR, NEW PRODUCTS

John Sandklev | ASSISTANT DIRECTOR, CONTINUITIES

Christopher Berzolla, Robert Fox, Michael Holahan, Amy Jacobsson,
Jennifer McLyman, Dan Melore | PRODUCT MANAGERS

Tom Mifsud | MANAGER, RETAIL AND NEW MARKETS

Alyse Daberko, Alison Ehrmann, Pamela Paul, Charlotte Siddiqui,
Dawn Weland | ASSOCIATE PRODUCT MANAGERS

Meredith Shelley, Betty Su | ASSISTANT PRODUCT MANAGERS

John Calvano | EDITORIAL OPERATIONS MANAGER

Michelle Gudema | FULFILLMENT DIRECTOR

Tricia Griffin | FINANCIAL MANAGER

Heather Lynds | ASSISTANT FINANCIAL MANAGER

Lyndsay Jenks | MARKETING ASSISTANT

CONSUMER MARKETING DIVISION

John E. Tighe | PRODUCTION DIRECTOR

Donna Miano-Ferrara | BOOK PRODUCTION MANAGER

Jessica McGrath | ASSISTANT BOOK PRODUCTION MANAGER

EDITOR IN CHIEF: Norman Pearlstine
EDITORIAL DIRECTOR: Henry Muller
EDITOR OF NEW MEDIA: Daniel Okrent

PRESIDENT, CEO: Don Logan
EXECUTIVE VICE PRESIDENTS: Elizabeth Valk Long,
Jim Nelson, Joseph A. Ripp

MANAGING EDITOR
James W. Seymore Jr.
EXECUTIVE EDITOR
Richard Sanders
ASSISTANT MANAGING EDITORS
Peter Bonventre, Jeannie Park
GENERAL EDITOR   DESIGN DIRECTOR
David Hajdu   John Korpics
PHOTOGRAPHY DIRECTOR   L.A. BUREAU CHIEF
Mary Dunn   Cable Neuhaus
PICTURE EDITOR
Doris Brautigan
SENIOR EDITORS: George Blooston, Doug Brod, Mark Harris,
Albert Kim, John McAlley, Maggie Murphy, Mary Kaye Schilling
SPECIAL PROJECTS EDITOR: Alison Gwinn
DIRECTOR OF RESEARCH SERVICES: Annabel Bentley

EDITORIAL MANAGER: Lauren Kunkler
STAFF EDITORS: Jamie Bufalino, Jess Cagle, Cynthia Grisolia, Tina Jordan
CRITIC-AT-LARGE: Ken Tucker
CRITICS: David Browne, Ty Burr, Bruce Fretts,
Owen Gleiberman, Lisa Schwarzbaum
WRITERS-AT-LARGE: Dana Kennedy, Benjamin Svetkey
SENIOR WRITERS: Rebecca Ascher-Walsh, Steve Daly, Joe Flint,
Jeff Gordinier, David Hochman, A.J. Jacobs, Gregg Kilday, Chris Willman
SENIOR ASSOCIATE EDITOR: Caren Weiner
ASSOCIATE EDITORS: Doug Brantley, Eileen Clarke, Marion Hart,
Dulcy Israel, Joe Neumaier, William Stevenson, Mitchell Vinicor, Tracy A. Walsh
STAFF WRITERS: Kate Meyers, Degen Pener, Tom Sinclair, Dan Snierson
CORRESPONDENTS: Kristen Baldwin, Dave Karger, Christopher Nashawaty,
Jessica Shaw
SENIOR BROADCAST CORRESPONDENT: Lisa Karlin

COPY
CHIEF: Ben Spier   DEPUTY: Steven Pearl

DESIGN
ASSOCIATE ART DIRECTORS: Joe Kimberling, Rina Migliaccio, John Walker
ASSISTANT ART DIRECTORS: Dirk Barnett, Bobby B. Lawhorn Jr.
DESIGNER: George McCalman
DESIGN ASSISTANT: Erin Whelan

PICTURES
PICTURE EDITOR, SPECIAL PROJECTS: Sarah Rozen
ASSOCIATE PICTURE EDITOR: Alice H. Babcock
ASSISTANT PICTURE EDITORS: Helena V. Ashton,
Michael Kochman (L.A.), Richard B. Maltz, Michele Romero
ASSISTANT: L. Michelle Dougherty

NEW MEDIA
COORDINATOR: Stan Olson

RESEARCH SERVICES
REPORTERS: Tim Purtell (Deputy), Louis Vogel (Senior Reporter),
Michelle Bowers, Jason Cochran, Kristi Huelsing, Beth Johnson, Cheo Tyehimba
INFORMATION CENTER MANAGER: Rachel Sapienza
DEPUTY: Stacie Fenster   ASSOCIATE: Sean O'Heir
ASSISTANT: Alexandria Carrion

PRODUCTION
MAKEUP MANAGER: Robin Kaplan
PLANT OPERATIONS MANAGER: Karen S. Doyle
PRODUCTION MANAGER: Sue Barnett
STAFF: Ray Battaglino, George L. Beke, Paul Bodley Jr.,
Kevin Christian, Evan J. Dong, John Goodman, Don Gordon,
Robert D. Kennedy, Bill Lazzarotti, Lisa DiSapio Motti,
Ann Griffith O'Connor, Lauren Planit, Eve A. Rabinovits,
Tom Roemlein, Leona Smith, George Sumerak, Daniel C. Thompson

TECHNOLOGY
MANAGER: James S. Mittelmark
SENIOR TECHNOLOGY COORDINATORS: Jeffrey Cherins, Godwin Mensah
TECHNOLOGY COORDINATOR: Joe Russell

EDITORIAL ASSISTANTS
Rob Brunner, Kipp Erante Cheng, Shirley Y. Fung, Anna Holmes, Alexandra
Jacobs, Tricia Laine, Erin Richter, Gary Eng Walk

ADMINISTRATION
ASSISTANT TO THE MANAGING EDITOR: Rita Silverstein
STAFF: Carole Willcocks

CONTRIBUTORS
Pat H. Broeske, Mike Flaherty, Vanessa V. Friedman, Nisid Hajari, L.S. Klepp,
Ann Kolson, Gene Lyons, Lois Alter Mark, Margot Mifflin, Jim Mullen, Alanna
Nash, Lawrence O'Toole, David Poland, Ira Robbins, Michael Sauter, Stephen
Schaefer, Heidi Siegmund Cuda, Bob Strauss

PRESIDENT
Michael J. Klingensmith
PUBLISHER: Michael J. Kelly
VICE PRESIDENT, CONSUMER MARKETING: Alexander H. Sareyan
CIRCULATION DIRECTOR: Monica Ray
DIRECTOR OF FINANCE & ADMINISTRATION: George H. Vollmuth
ASSOCIATE PUBLISHER: David S. Morris
PRODUCTION DIRECTOR: Carol A. Mazzarella
VICE PRESIDENT, ENTERTAINMENT MARKETING &
NEW BUSINESS DEVELOPMENT: Deanna C. Brown
ASSOCIATE PUBLISHER: Daniel J. Osheyack
DIRECTOR OF PROMOTION AND PUBLIC AFFAIRS: Sandy W. Drayton
TIME INC.
EXECUTIVE EDITORS: Joëlle Attinger, José M. Ferrer III
DEVELOPMENT EDITOR: Isolde Motley
TIME INC. EDITORIAL SERVICES
DIRECTOR: Sheldon Czapnik
GENERAL MANAGER: Claude Boral   PHOTO LAB: Thomas E. Hubbard
RESEARCH CENTER: Lany Walden McDonald
PICTURE COLLECTION: Beth Bencini Zarcone
TECHNOLOGY: Thomas Smith   MARKETING: James Macove
TIME INC. EDITORIAL TECHNOLOGY
VICE PRESIDENT: Paul Zazzera   DIRECTOR: Damien Creavin

In the following pages, you'll find the 100 supernovas grouped according to category (The Leading Men, Sex Goddesses, Tough Guys, Ingenues...). But, in case you were wondering, here's how we would rank them, 1 to 100:

1. Humphrey Bogart
2. Katharine Hepburn
3. Jimmy Stewart
4. Marilyn Monroe
5. John Wayne
6. Cary Grant
7. Marlon Brando
8. Clark Gable
9. Charlie Chaplin
10. Bette Davis
11. Elizabeth Taylor
12. Ingrid Bergman
13. Paul Newman
14. James Cagney
15. Spencer Tracy
16. Clint Eastwood
17. Jack Nicholson
18. Gary Cooper
19. Fred Astaire
20. Laurence Olivier
21. Audrey Hepburn
22. James Dean
23. Judy Garland
24. Sean Connery
25. Greta Garbo
26. Tom Hanks
27. Grace Kelly
28. Dustin Hoffman

29. Henry Fonda
30. Robert Redford
31. Tom Cruise
32. Rudolph Valentino
33. Jack Lemmon
34. Robert De Niro
35. Buster Keaton
36. Kirk Douglas
37. Meryl Streep
38. Shirley Temple
39. Burt Lancaster
40. Barbara Stanwyck
41. Al Pacino
42. Gene Kelly
43. Marlene Dietrich
44. Sidney Poitier
45. Laurel & Hardy
46. Harrison Ford
47. Joan Crawford
48. Mel Gibson
49. Jean Harlow
50. Robin Williams
51. Jane Fonda
52. Charlton Heston
53. Arnold Schwarzenegger
54. Barbra Streisand
55. Errol Flynn
56. Steve McQueen
57. Jodie Foster
58. Gregory Peck
59. Frank Sinatra
60. Montgomery Clift
61. Robert Mitchum
62. The Marx Brothers
63. William Holden
64. John Travolta
65. Rita Hayworth
66. Edward G. Robinson
67. Michelle Pfeiffer

68. Douglas Fairbanks Sr.
69. Mary Pickford
70. Natalie Wood
71. Michael Douglas
72. Doris Day
73. Lillian Gish
74. Rock Hudson
75. Vivien Leigh
76. Bing Crosby
77. Warren Beatty
78. Richard Burton
79. Faye Dunaway
80. Sylvester Stallone
81. Lon Chaney
82. Kevin Costner
83. Olivia de Havilland
84. Woody Allen
85. Sophia Loren
86. Carole Lombard
87. Jessica Lange
88. Ava Gardner
89. Bob Hope
90. Julia Roberts
91. Peter O'Toole
92. Eddie Murphy
93. Susan Sarandon
94. Sharon Stone
95. Brigitte Bardot
96. Julie Andrews
97. Bruce Willis
98. Denzel Washington
99. Anthony Hopkins
100. Susan Hayward

Let us now have a moment of silence in memory of Florence Lawrence.

Don't know who she is? That's okay—audiences early in 1909 didn't know either. She was simply "the Biograph girl," an actress who appeared in short films made by the Biograph company of New York. But later that year, when producer Carl Laemmle noted the volume of mail the still-anonymous Lawrence was receiving and signed her to the company that would eventually become Universal Pictures, he began to promote her—by name—in a series of outrageous publicity stunts, including a rumor that she had been run over by a streetcar. Within months, Florence Lawrence was transformed into something then unheard of: the first movie star.

With her ascendancy, Lawrence turned the neophyte film industry on its head, creating the real currency of Hollywood—the stars themselves—and leading indirectly to the screen royalty celebrated in this book. She was the first proof that we go to the cinema not simply to see movies but to marvel at the people in them.

We marvel because they make aspects of ourselves available for communal dreaming, writ large and luminous on a theater wall. All civilizations need gods to worship: The Romans had Mars and Minerva; the Norse had Thor and Odin. The present age is different only in its choice of church: The multiplex is our temple, and the great stars are our sources of aspiration. That they're human only makes them more fascinating, as if Zeus had come to earth with a SAG card.

The 100 stars ranked here are legends not necessarily because they are the greatest actors, or made the best movies, or stayed the longest at the feast. Each is here because he or she created (or is continuing to create) a unique personality, bigger than any single film—bigger, often, than the man or woman behind the makeup. It's impossible to imagine the movies without Audrey Hepburn's elegant fire, Spencer Tracy's unmannered grit, Marlene Dietrich's kinky opacity, Laurel & Hardy's infantile brilliance.

These and the other actors from Hollywood's Golden Age—the early '30s through the late '50s—are the inevitables on this list because so many of them had the luxury of long, rich careers. We framed the criteria differently when it came to the stars of the '70s, '80s, and '90s. Michelle Pfeiffer or Robin Williams cannot rightly be called a "legend" on the order of Bogie or Kate Hepburn. Not yet—maybe not ever. But we sought to pay tribute to those current performers who seem to be at least halfway there, who have created something entirely new or given fresh twists to the old archetypes.

We've organized this book along more generic playing styles, dividing our 100 into the 11 essential Hollywood character types. Again, they fill a very human need that goes back to the dawn of storytelling. Just as ancient Greeks had their god of war, we have our action heroes; as African pantheisms had their tricksters, we have our

his or her image. Some favorite movies may not be included here; there are others you may never have heard of. All speak to the drama of their subjects' careers.

By far the hardest part of this project was limiting ourselves to an even 100. The names that didn't quite make the list—often the subject of vociferous debate among the writers and editors at ENTERTAINMENT WEEKLY who worked on this project—could make up an alternate Greatest Stars book. Woody Allen, but not Orson Welles? (Yes, because the former was an actor first, while the latter was always primarily a director.) Judy Garland, but not Mickey Rooney? (She's the classic gifted victim of the system; he, merely an astonished survivor.) Where are Claudette Colbert, Charles Boyer,

If the cinema is our temple, then these are our gods and goddesses: the 100 stars who've left an unforgettable imprint on the screen

great comedians; the temptresses of long-ago epics are the sex goddesses of today. Looming above them all are the members of the Hollywood pantheon: 10 actors and actresses who coined cinematic personae so particular, so irreducible, so alluring that they transcend types. Rather, by their evanescent nature, they define—as much as anything can define—what it is to be a star.

In addition, for each of the 100 stars we have chosen the key films and explained why they matter. With the coming of home video, entire filmographies are available for rental, but rare is the video store that highlights the best Gregory Peck movies, say, or the essential Marilyn Monroe. So consider these accompanying lists a crash course in Stardom 101, including films that created new celebrities, films in which stars rose to further heights, and—often the most interesting—films in which an idol tried to alter or deepen

Lana Turner, Betty Grable, Ray Milland? You're right; they're deserving. But the ultimate test was, Did the actor or actress create an on-screen persona that lives on in our culture both as a type (a John Wayne-style hero) and as an inimitable singularity (John Wayne)?

In truth, when earnestness and wit and art and commerce commingle, and the results are as fine as, say, 'Jerry Maguire' or 'Pulp Fiction' or 'The English Patient,' it seems as if we could be entering a new golden age of stars. Whom does the next generation belong to? For one possibility, look to a recent Romeo and Juliet, Leonardo DiCaprio and Claire Danes. He could be played by a young James Dean, she by Natalie Wood. Don't laugh: Every actor in this issue was scorned as an upstart pretender at some point in his or her career. Florence Lawrence notwithstanding, we grow our idols slowly. We also grow them big. —Ty Burr

THE 10 PERFORMERS in our first chapter signal the creation of a new breed of larger-than-life archetypes. With the earliest of these performers, Charlie Chaplin, you can actually see the evolution—from stage to screen, from shtick to stardom—take place.

These essential screen personalities set the mold for virtually every other star in this book, but at bottom, the Top Ten are inimitable. Think of all the matinee idols and party impressionists over the years who have tried to "do" Cary Grant; think of how comically they have fallen short.

It's impossible to do Cary Grant, of course, because Cary Grant just is. His persona owes something to previous leading men, but the whole unnaturally alert package is a quicksilver distillation of what modern civilized man could be. The same goes for the trenchant disillusionment of Bogart, the equine allure of Kate Hepburn,

The Top Ten

the cautious gregariousness of Jimmy Stewart, the manly ease of Gable, Wayne's swaggering grace, Davis' incandescent frenzy—all natural outgrowths of personalities that became, somehow, both instantaneous and timeless on a 40-foot screen. Marilyn Monroe and Marlon Brando may be the odd ducks here, in that she summed up several generations of earlier blond movie vamps while he destroyed the notion of star-as-product by insisting on star-as-process. Both have been imitated beyond absurdity, but it is the ease of presentation that sets them apart and above. That ease has seemed impossible to come by in real life—for Brando almost as tragically as for Monroe, and for many of the others as well. If nothing else, here is lasting proof of accomplishment: that performers racked by professional and personal insecurity were able to create vivid, complete mythical beings. Yes, they are inimitable—that's why we want to be like them. –Ty Burr

'The Philadelphia Story' caught three Top Ten stars at the top of their game. The film gave Katharine Hepburn a much-needed comeback role, brought Stewart his only Oscar, and solidified Cary Grant as the ultimate leading man. Watch the 1940 film today and you realize why certain stars never go out of style.

1

Humphrey

Bogart

"Himself, he never took too seriously—his work, most seriously. He regarded the somewhat gaudy figure of Bogart, the star, with amused cynicism; Bogart, the actor, he held in deep respect." JOHN HUSTON

IN THE 1960S, college students rediscovered Humphrey Bogart by way of film societies and the late-late show; he became, in effect, the one old-time movie star this new generation felt it could trust. At the risk of sounding sacrilegious, it is probably a good thing the actor was dead by then. It's not that the mythical Bogie—the last honest man punching with surly nobility at whatever authority presented itself—wasn't worthy of worship. It's just that the myth was—and is—so powerful that the real Bogart could never have lived up to his new fans' expectations. It took a lifelong career, in fact, even to convince himself that he was that man.

Think about it: Bogart was the least known of the Broadway performers snapped up by the movie studios when sound came in. Jimmy Cagney and Edward G. Robinson slipped naturally into gangster roles, and Spencer Tracy was already known as a searing actor's actor. Bogart, by contrast, was the quintessential romantic juvenile—the kid who shows up in the first act holding a tennis racket. The actress Louise Brooks remembers the young Bogart in her memoirs as a "slim boy with charming manners, who was unusually quiet for an actor." Bogart's first film roles made no impression on audiences, and he returned to Broadway, where he was cast as a vicious thug named Duke Mantee in 'The Petrified Forest.' He took the role to Hollywood in 1936, and Bogie was born. But not yet perfected—not turned into the burnt, rebellious cynic of our dreams. Bogart played a lot of gangsters in the '30s, usually the sniveling rat who gets his comeuppance at Cagney's gunpoint. He was miscast in romances (an Irish stable man opposite Bette Davis in 'Dark Victory') and Westerns (the wonderfully ridicu-lous 'Oklahoma Kid'). It was 1941's 'High Sierra' that pulled the pieces together; Bogart played an aging gangster for sympathy rather than hisses, and suddenly those weary basset-hound eyes conveyed a new worldliness.

Unlike most Hollywood actors, Bogart was better suited to middle age than youth, and in the films of his peak years—'The Maltese Falcon' (1941), 'Casablanca' (1942), 'To Have and Have Not' (1944), 'The Big Sleep' (1946), and 'The Treasure of the Sierra Madre' (1948)— he conveyed the wry gravity of one who has seen it all and doesn't care, at least until the moment when Ilsa shows up at Rick's. By this point it was clear that Bogart was trying hard to be Bogie in real life. His compatriots confirmed it in quote after quote, the most famous being restaurateur Dave Chasen's comment that "Bogart's a helluva nice guy until 11:30 p.m. After that, he thinks he's Bogart."

Few were allowed behind the facade—fourth wife Lauren Bacall, not many others. Only two movies dared to penetrate the myth: In Nicholas Ray's 'In a Lonely Place' (1950) and the more stolid 'Caine Mutiny' (1954), the Bogie toughness devolves into a horrible, soul-killing paranoia. By then, he knew the character well enough to parody it—and won his only Oscar (for 1951's 'The African Queen') doing so. He died in 1957 at the age of 57, too early but with nothing much left to prove. His job was done. Bogie lives. (Photograph by Philippe Halsman) —TB

Katharine Hepburn

IT WASN'T the most memorable of the 44 feature films Katharine Hepburn has made, but the title of her 1936 Victorian-era drama, 'A Woman Rebels,' perfectly expresses her appeal. Throughout the '30s and '40s, Hepburn was as much a life force as she was an actress—an extraordinary package of beauty, culture, brains, wit, grace, strength, and, above all, spirit. She was the original liberated woman, on and off the screen, tilting at the windmills of convention and male dominance.

Hepburn was born to independence. Her father was a prosperous Hartford, Conn., urologist who corresponded with Mrs. George Bernard Shaw; her mother crusaded for women's suffrage. The day after Hepburn graduated from Bryn Mawr in 1928, she joined a Baltimore stock company, and by the end of the year, she was appearing on Broadway. By her own admission, though, she was not a very good actress, far more temperamental than talented. It wasn't until 1932 that she made a favorable impression, as a scantily clad Amazon in 'The Warrior's Husband.' Hollywood came calling, in the person of RKO's David O. Selznick, but Hepburn, who declared, "They didn't like me until I got into a leg show," tried to chase him off by demanding $1,500 a week. To her surprise, Selznick agreed.

Hepburn proved to be worth it. Her first film, 'A Bill of Divorcement' (1932), was a critical and box office success, and it began her long, fruitful association with director George Cukor. For only her third picture, 'Morning Glory,' she won the 1933 Best Actress Oscar. She earned the second of her record 12 Oscar nominations for 'Alice Adams' (1935); the next year she gave an Oscar-worthy performance as the cross-dressing Sylvia/Sylvester in 'Sylvia Scarlett,' but this Cukor film was so ahead of its time that it went unappreciated. The picture, though, did pair Hepburn for the first time with Cary Grant.

The playful Grant and the patrician Hepburn were a perfect match in two classic 1938 comedies, Howard Hawks' screwball 'Bringing Up Baby' and Cukor's sophisticated 'Holiday.' When playwright Philip Barry wrote 'The Philadelphia Story' with Hepburn in mind, she agreed to do it on Broadway in exchange for the movie rights, which she sold to MGM on the condition that Cukor direct. Grant costarred, along with Jimmy Stewart. The 1940 film brought Hepburn a third nomination.

In '42 she met a new match in Spencer Tracy, her costar in the newsroom comedy 'Woman of the Year.' As the story goes, when Hepburn encountered the older actor, she said, "I think you're a little short for me," to which producer Joe Mankiewicz replied, "Don't worry, he'll cut you down to size." The movie was a huge success. Hepburn and Tracy made eight more films together—'Adam's Rib' and 'Pat and Mike' were the best of those—while off screen they conducted a discreet, 25-year affair.

Hepburn did make a fair number of duds ('Spitfire,' 'Dragon Seed'). But when she was good, she was very, very good; and those performances usually came opposite actors who challenged her—Grant, Tracy, and, in John Huston's 'The African Queen' (1951), Humphrey Bogart. "She does pretty much as she goddamn pleases," Bogart once said of his costar. "You never pull up a chair for Kate. You tell her, 'Kate, pull me up a chair, willya, and while you're at it get one for yourself.' I don't think she tries to be a character. I think she is one." (Photograph by Bob Henriques) —Steve Wulf

ESSENTIAL HEPBURN

ALICE ADAMS
(1935, above) She's eerily beautiful, exasperatingly silly, and, finally, moving as a small-town girl desperate for respect.

BRINGING UP BABY
(1938) In a peerlessly manic Howard Hawks screwball comedy, she woos Cary Grant by driving him nuts.

THE PHILADELPHIA STORY
(1940) The lady's finest hour, with a tailor-made script and perfect-match support from Grant and Jimmy Stewart.

WOMAN OF THE YEAR
(1942, above) A ravishingly lovely Hepburn meets a down-to-earth Spencer Tracy, and a wonderful on-screen marriage begins.

THE AFRICAN QUEEN
(1951) Parodying her own starchy Yankee persona as a minister's sister who finds unexpected love upriver with Bogie.

Jimmy Stewart

3

POOR JIMMY STEWART was everybody's favorite movie buddy, boyfriend, father, and uncle for so long that his real gifts as an actor were buried under a landslide of national affection. Even Harry Truman said, "If Bess and I had a son, we'd want him to be just like Jimmy Stewart." We respond to his characters' folksy stammer, his small-town modesty, the eyes that light up in naive yet purposeful passion, because we so want to believe such goodness is something all Americans share.

This is the Stewart of Frank Capra flicks—of 'Mr. Smith Goes to Washington' (1939) and the beloved, over-exposed 'It's a Wonderful Life' (1946)—but it is only part of the story. George Cukor's 'The Philadelphia Story' (1940) and Ernst Lubitsch's 'The Shop Around the Corner' (1940) are romantic comedies that show a smarter, more peevish Jimmy, and after World War II he made several Westerns with director Anthony Mann ('Bend of the River,' 'The Naked Spur') that are remarkable for the bitter maturity he reveals. Later came the rich films with Hitchcock, particularly 'Rear Window' (1954) and the truly kinky 'Vertigo' (1958), in which Stewart leads us into voyeurism, obsession, and beyond. In retrospect, his key movie is 'Wonderful Life' not because it makes us feel so good, but because he makes George Bailey's despair so harrowingly real. Until the end he remained a tower of affability, but as an actor he was more fascinating as he became less wholesome. —TB

Marilyn Monroe

IF HALF OF AMERICA wanted to take advantage of her, then the other half wanted to take care of her. The country was transfixed by this gossamer creature with a body built for lust and a soul steeped in sorrow. Though her turbulent offscreen life often spilled over into filming, it also turned up her box office heat—and our fascination with her has yet to cool down.

Monroe was a mass of contradictions: pliant yet demanding, intelligent yet ditsy, outwardly bubbly yet inwardly depressed. It's little wonder: She was blessed with sex appeal and cursed by her upbringing. Her mother, Gladys Mortenson, spent much of her adult life in mental institutions, forcing Norma Jean to live in a succession of foster homes and, for two formative years, an orphanage. She would spend the rest of her life compensating for the pain and confusion of those early years.

In 1950, four years after signing her first Hollywood contract, Marilyn's agent and lover, Johnny Hyde, helped her land small but scene-stealing roles in 'The Asphalt Jungle' and 'All About Eve,' and her career began to take off: 'Don't Bother to Knock' (1952), in which she played a psychotic babysitter; 'Niagara' (1953), which prompted one critic to opine, "The falls and Miss Monroe are something to see"; and 'Gentlemen Prefer Blondes' (1953), for which she provided the proof of the pudding. Throughout most of her career, she was high maintenance, what with her moods, her substance abuse, and her ever-present coaches. And her love life was a constant source of personal suffering and public intrigue:

"She was so adorable, so witty, such incredible fun and more physically attractive than anyone I could have imagined apart from herself on the screen"
LAURENCE OLIVIER

She couldn't have picked two more diverse husbands than baseball great Joe DiMaggio and Pulitzer Prize-winning playwright Arthur Miller. That both marriages ended so calamitously only added to her tragic myth.

Monroe's best roles, by and large, were slight variations on her status as a siren. In 'The Seven Year Itch' (1955), she plays the upstairs object of Tom Ewell's fantasy. In 'Bus Stop' (1956), Monroe weaves "That Old Black Magic" so well that she deserved at least an Oscar nomination—an honor she never received. And in 'Some Like It Hot' (1959), her ukulele-playing Sugar Kane is both hilarious and heartrending—the girlfriends she finally finds are Tony Curtis and Jack Lemmon.

There was deception in her life as well. She was used by "friends" and lovers, and even a President. (It's hard separating Marilyn from her Cherie in 'Bus Stop,' who says, "I just got to feel that whoever I marry has some real regard for me, aside from all that lovin' stuff.") Her drug overdose in 1962 now seems almost inevitable. But at least she died a star. As Billy Wilder, the director she bedeviled in both 'The Seven Year Itch' and 'Some Like It Hot,' said after her death, "There never has been a face with such voltage on the screen with the exception of Garbo. We just happen to miss her like hell." (Photograph by Milton H. Greene) —SW

4

John Wayne

5

EIGHTEEN YEARS after his death, Wayne is still so tangled up in this country's culture wars that it's impossible to have a rational conversation about him. There are people who refuse to watch his movies; there are others who refuse to watch anything but. The problem is that Wayne embodies certain American qualities so well that one's response to him is, by default, political. His moral certainty can look like pigheaded reactionism, his reliance on the physical like the mark of a bully, his terseness like smug insensitivity, his cowboy boosterism like bigotry.

What gets lost in the battle is how consciously Wayne the actor addressed those contradictions in his roles. From his breakthrough to stardom with 'Stagecoach' (1939) to his lovely, quiet swan song, 'The Shootist' (1976), Wayne built a body of work that examines what it is to be a hero in America. No one who actually sits down and watches 'Red River' (1948) or 'The Searchers' (1956) can doubt Wayne knew the pitfalls of power and obsession that plagued the men he played, and his filmography is studded with as much bitterness (1945's 'They Were Expendable') as strength (1959's 'Rio Bravo'). To demonize Wayne—or idolize him—is to cheat him out of his real complexity. Worse, to miss his movies is to cheat yourself. (Photograph by Phil Stern) —TB

"He gave the whole world the image of what an American should be"
ELIZABETH TAYLOR

Cary Grant 6

IF HOLLYWOOD had its own Mount Rushmore, Cary Grant's profile would be the most prominent: the hair that Katharine Hepburn mussed in 'Bringing Up Baby' (1938), the lips that locked with Ingrid Bergman's in 'Notorious' (1946), the eyes that Eva Marie Saint couldn't quite meet in 'North by Northwest' (1959), and, of course, the cleft chin that fascinated Audrey Hepburn in 'Charade' (1963). Born into poverty in England as Archibald Alexander Leach, he ran away from home at 13 to join an acrobatic troupe as a juggler. That may explain why, once he found his way to Hollywood, Grant could perform with equal aplomb the tricks of comedy, suspense, action, and romance. He graced 73 films in 34 years, and the fact that he never won an Academy Award makes a mockery of the Oscars. He certainly deserved one for 'Notorious,' in which he plays a spy conflicted by his love for Bergman. Though Grant was the very picture of urbanity, one could always sense the turmoil simmering beneath the surface. "I have spent the greater part of my life fluctuating between Archie Leach and Cary Grant," he once said, "unsure of each, suspecting each." Unlike Grant, his audience was willing to embrace them both. — SW

Marlon Brando 7

HE WAS HANDSOME ENOUGH to be a heartthrob, tough enough to play a mug, and gifted enough to challenge Laurence Olivier as the greatest actor who ever lived. But with his brooding slouch and muttered Method line readings, Marlon Brando was unlike any other leading man Hollywood had ever seen. He was more intense, more animalistic—and more iconoclastic. "What are you rebelling against?" somebody asks him in 'The Wild One' (1954). Brando's answer: "What have you got?" Pauline Kael once described him as "a Byronic Dead End Kid"—referring, of course, to the early Brando, whose angry young antiheroes (like Stanley Kowalski in 1951's 'A Streetcar Named Desire' and Terry Malloy in 1954's 'On the Waterfront,' for which he earned his first Best Actor Oscar) grabbed the attention of young postwar Americans and inspired at least two generations of acting descendants. Brando's fire may have simmered down in later years, but not that rebellious streak. He's never settled for doing the expected or the accepted, whether that meant playing Fletcher Christian as an effeminate fop in 'Mutiny on the Bounty' (1962) or toppling taboos in the sexually explicit 'Last Tango in Paris' (1973).

More recently, Brando has contented himself with doing high-priced cameos in commercial fluff. His disdain for Hollywood's creative decline is understandable yet lamentable: If only he'd chosen to set a good example instead, there's no telling how many more great performances he might have given. But who knows? He may surprise us yet. — Michael Sauter

ESSENTIAL
GRANT

SYLVIA SCARLETT
(1936) After several years of drab roles, Grant blossomed into, well, Cary Grant, opposite Kate Hepburn in comic drag.

BRINGING UP BABY
(1938) Maybe the most maddeningly funny screwball comedy of all, with Grant a fuddled paleontologist chased by ditsy Hepburn.

HIS GIRL FRIDAY
(1940) In the revamped 'Front Page,' he delivers as the most devious, fast-talking, hilarious newspaper editor ever put on film.

NOTORIOUS
(1946) Grant woos gorgeous Ingrid Bergman for love and country in Hitchcock's deliriously romantic suspense masterpiece.

NORTH BY NORTHWEST
(1959) Crisscrossing the country, ducking crop dusters, and hanging from Mount Rushmore as a Manhattan exec caught in a spy plot.

ESSENTIAL BRANDO

A STREETCAR NAMED DESIRE
(1951) Nearly 50 years on, Brando's brutish Stanley Kowalski still conveys the shock that launched a revolution in acting.

ON THE WATERFRONT
(1954) Indelible and unforgettable as palooka Terry Malloy, a thug who gradually grows a conscience on the docks of Hoboken.

THE WILD ONE
(1954) This tawdry biker drama ain't the greatest movie, but it's an essential '50s document and a quintessential Brando role.

THE GODFATHER
(1972) He won his second Oscar for a midlife performance that's a triumph of cold technique—cotton wadding and all.

LAST TANGO IN PARIS
(1973) Ignore the notoriety: Brando is deeply harrowing as a man trying to erase sorrow and self through anonymous sex.

Charlie Chaplin

FOR THE GREATEST part of this century Charlie Chaplin was one of the most recognizable human beings on the planet. At 17, he joined a comedy troupe that took him from London to America, where he signed up with slapstick-movie maven Mack Sennett for $150 a week. His subsequent popularity can be tracked by his paycheck: In 1915, he jumped to the Essanay studio for $1,250 a week; in 1916, to Mutual for $10,000 a week; in 1918, to First National for an unheard-of $150,000 per short.

With 1921's huge success, 'The Kid,' his heart-tugging became overt, and Chaplin morphed from incredibly gifted comedian to allegorical figure: '1984' author George Orwell lauded "his power to stand for a sort of concentrated essence of the common man." You don't read comments like that and not have them go to your head. The '20s and '30s saw Chaplin's most indelible moments—eating the shoe in 'The Gold Rush,' the close-up at the end of 'City Lights,' caught in the cogs of 'Modern Times'—yet it was clear he was retreating behind a wall of global adulation and transfixed self-regard.

Since his death in 1977, his stock has fallen a bit. His sentimentality now looks quaint, Victorian, out of touch. All perhaps true, and all moot when you witness the rich, melancholy funniness of his best work. Chaplin set the mold for the comic who does not feel complete until he is accepted as an artist; in so doing, he paved the way for everyone from Jerry Lewis to Woody Allen to Robin Williams. Unlike them—unlike anybody else—he got the entire world to agree. (Photograph by Edward Steichen) —TB

Clark Gable

THEY CALLED HIM the King; they needed one just then. If Shirley Temple reassured Depression audiences that innocence still existed, Gable gave them proof of ongoing male strength. In fact, he was a one-man revolution in masculinity: After the playful decadence of the Roaring '20s, Hollywood had filled the newly talking screen with wooden tenors and twee Broadway boys. Gable came from the stage too, but his dangerous sexuality was made for the intimacy of film. After an incredible 12 movies in 1931, his first year at MGM, he was so pervasive that the hip put-down was "Who do you think you are—Clark Gable?"

His status as Hollywood's own Jove was sealed with 'Gone With the Wind' (1939), and both Rhett's marital rape of Scarlett and his don't-give-a-damn adieu still pack a transgressive shock. But Gable seems never to have gotten over the death of his third wife, Carole Lombard, in a 1942 plane crash, and his postwar roles show uncertainty peeping out from behind that dimpled ease. Still, the legend held until the last. On starring with him in his last movie, 'The Misfits' (1961), Marilyn Monroe said, "Can you imagine what being kissed by him meant to me?" (Photograph by Bob Landry) —TB

ESSENTIAL CHAPLIN

ONE A.M.
(1916) A slapstick short of breathtaking bravura: one set (a suburban home), one performer (Chaplin, as a drunk coming home), hundreds of gags.

THE GOLD RUSH
(1925) After polishing his Little Tramp persona in years of two-reelers, he hit his feature-film stride with this hilarious Alaskan epic.

CITY LIGHTS
(1931) Sentiment and slapstick mingle as the Tramp enters the boxing ring for the love of a blind girl.

MODERN TIMES
(1936) As a little guy who gets chewed up by assembly-line gears, Chaplin had his best on-screen femme foil in wife Paulette Goddard.

MONSIEUR VERDOUX
(1947) Far too grim for '40s audiences, this modern-day Bluebeard comedy has become Chaplin's dark classic.

ESSENTIAL GABLE

RED DUST
(1932) As a rubber-plantation hunk, Gable has his choice of slinky Jean Harlow and elegant Mary Astor. All men should be so lucky.

IT HAPPENED ONE NIGHT
(1934) Playing a cocky reporter on the road with heiress Claudette Colbert, he's the early-'30s idea of manly perfection.

MUTINY ON THE BOUNTY
(1935) When Captain Bligh is nasty Charles Laughton and Christian is Gable with his shirt off, whom are you going to side with?

GONE WITH THE WIND
(1939) ``My reaction to Rhett,'' said Gable, ``was immediate and enthusiastic: `What a part for Ronald Colman.'''

THE MISFITS
(1961) In this flawed anti-Western, his last performance, Gable finally stretches—and grabs the gold ring.

"Bette Davis taught Hollywood to follow an actress instead of the actress following the camera, and she's probably the best movie actress there's ever been"
ELAINE STRITCH

Bette Davis

SHE ONCE TOLD a reporter that the reason she worked so hard was that there were so few real actresses in films—and there you have the feral ambition of a woman who is certain of her own worth yet knows she is not "pretty." Stardom, for Davis, was a protracted war: against her bosses at Warner Bros., against rival actresses, against the two-dimensionality of most women's roles. "Until you're known in my profession as a monster, you're not a star," she once said, and she said it with grim satisfaction.

The public loved her for it: Davis was a top box office draw throughout the '30s and '40s, and in 1948 she was the highest-paid star in Hollywood. By then she had amassed a gallery of antiheroines notable for their scalding intensity: a vicious tart in 'Of Human Bondage' (1934), a witchy Southern belle in 'Jezebel' (1938), the murdering adulteress of 'The Letter' (1940). "No one is as good as Bette when she's bad," gurgled the posters for 'In This Our Life' (1942), but they missed the point—not to mention the gift for worldly comedy Davis would show off in 1950's 'All About Eve,' for which she earned her eighth of 10 Oscar nominations. Davis' women—good or bad—are about strength, and the thwarted will behind the strength. To the women in the back row of the Bijou, she was one of their own. (Photograph by Walt Sanders) —TB

10

John W. Considine, Jr. *presents*

RUDOLPH VALENTINO

in

"The Son of the Sheik"

a Sequel to "The Sheik"

Leading the Men

THE TIMES ARE tough right now for the conventional Hollywood leading man. In a self-reflexively arch culture in which every action has its attendant smirk, unironic heroism seems downright dull. Maybe it's the lingering fallout of the '60s counterculture—in which leaders were distrusted by default—but we tend to follow the class clown these days rather than the class president.

And yet the matinee idols in these pages have made it work for them, through sexiness, class, and a no-nonsense belief in what they are doing. For some, the appeal lies in their ability to wink at the audience—like Paul Newman and the post-comeback John Travolta—but most convey a charisma rooted in earnest assurance. That's a tight suit to wear, and it has hindered some of the actors here. Robert Redford may never have played anyone as deeply thoughtful as he himself seems to be; Denzel Washington only rarely lets his wit flash on screen; Rock Hudson simply divided his life into two parts, one on display, the other obscured.

The two who may best represent the possibilities and pleasures of the breed come from opposite ends of movie history. Rudolph Valentino burst out of nowhere, driving women to frenzies of desire and expiring like a mayfly before age or the microphone could do him in. Tom Cruise, on the other hand, is the only classic leading man working today—classic in that he embodies noble, uninflected heroism. Intriguingly, he seems intent on seeing how such qualities carry into middle age. The species may be endangered, but the remaining specimens are intent on survival.—Ty Burr

"YOU GOT TO have balls and you got to have brains," Eddie Felson (Paul Newman) tells his protégé (Tom Cruise) in 1986's 'The Color of Money,' revealing the secret of pool hustling—and acting. You got to have looks, too, and audiences have marveled at Newman's ever since he scored his first big knockout as Rocky Graziano in 'Somebody Up There Likes Me' (1956). In 1958 alone Newman starred in 'The Left-Handed Gun' (as Billy the Kid), 'Rally 'Round the Flag, Boys!,' 'The Long Hot Summer,' and—in the first of his eight Best Actor-nominated roles—as Brick in 'Cat on a Hot Tin Roof.'

Newman is arguably the best actor of his generation because of other assets: the courage he displayed playing antiheroes (1961's 'The Hustler,' 1963's 'Hud') and the intelligence he gave his characters (1977's 'Slap Shot,' 1994's 'Nobody's Fool'). But what really made everyone out there like him was that he became the rebel with a cause. As Cool Hand Luke or Butch Cassidy, Newman gave his audiences a vicarious thrill by thumbing his nose at an unjust society. His 1986 Oscar for 'The Color of Money' was way overdue—he should have won it for 'The Hustler'—but at least it validated his real worth. It wasn't the blue eyes. It was the red blood and the gray matter. (Photograph by Sanford Roth)—Steve Wulf

Paul
Newman

ESSENTIAL NEWMAN

THE HUSTLER
(1961, above) A defining smart-young-stud performance as Fast Eddie Felson, cool pool kid cuing up against Minnesota Fats (Jackie Gleason).

HUD
(1963) Newman busts through a schematic script with honeyed amorality as a rancher's no-account son.

COOL HAND LUKE
(1967, below) The star definitely didn't have a failure to communicate as a blue-eyed, egg-eating chain-gang rebel.

SLAP SHOT
(1977) Hilarious as a small-time hockey player, Newman makes this underrated comedy a foul-mouthed gem.

THE VERDICT
(1982) As a burnt-out Boston lawyer who rediscovers his conscience at a price, he found one of his last great roles. So far.

Rudolph

Valentino

IN A FILM CAREER that spanned just six years, Valentino became the definitive Latin lover—and Hollywood's first male sex symbol. When Valentino fixed his lustful gaze on his screen paramours, women fainted in the darkened aisles. When he churned out a volume of insipid verse, it was snapped up by the thousands. And when he died, grieving hordes nearly rioted at his funeral.

A onetime taxi dancer and petty thief, Valentino first tangoed his way into female hearts in 'The Four Horsemen of the Apocalypse' (1921). That same year he starred in 'The Sheik'—the film that sealed his sensuous image, launched a craze for all things Arabian, and hinted at his own inner conflict. Like his Sheik character—an indolent, effeminate pasha who also looms as a potential rapist—Valentino was a paradox: The supreme lover, it was rumored, never consummated his first marriage and was utterly dominated in his second by a wife who was herself thought to be gay. (Indeed, his male detractors derided him, famously, as the Pink Powder Puff.) But scandal was cut short by his sudden death, caused by complications from a perforated ulcer, at age 31, in 1926. The resultant hysteria proved that when it came to inspiring fierce devotion, nobody did it better. —Nisid Hajari

ESSENTIAL VALENTINO

THE FOUR HORSEMEN OF THE APOCALYPSE
(1921) A hard-hitting antiwar drama—with a dance scene that turned Rudy into a star overnight.

THE SHEIK
(1921) Campy now, but when desert chieftain Valentino kidnapped Agnes Ayres for illicit pleasure, audiences fainted en masse.

BLOOD AND SAND
(1922, below) He simmered and steamed as a bullfighter going mano a womano against vamp Nita Naldi.

THE EAGLE
(1925) A lavishly produced Russian Robin Hood saga, it now looks to be Valentino's single best film.

SON OF THE SHEIK
(1926, below) His last movie is an action-packed improvement on the original, with Rudy enjoyably droll as both father and son.

ESSENTIAL CRUISE

RISKY BUSINESS
(1983) His breakthrough, as a suburban teen who matures in ways unexpected when he meets a hard-edged call girl (Rebecca De Mornay).

TOP GUN
(1986) MTV-style dogfights and Cruise's can-do charisma sold this one like process cheese. Which is pretty much what it was.

RAIN MAN
(1988) Our delight at Hoffman's meticulous craft obscures Cruise's equally strong turn as Raymond Babbitt's scheming brother.

BORN ON THE FOURTH OF JULY
(1989) The star is in virtually every frame of Ron Kovic's life story, changing from all-American boy to dignified paraplegic antiwar activist.

JERRY MAGUIRE
(1996) The prototypical Cruise role—a slick sports agent who learns to care— somehow becomes the one in which Tom at last looks life-size.

ESSENTIAL POITIER

THE DEFIANT ONES
(1958) "I been mad all my natural life," his convict sneers. At this point in his career, you could believe it.

LILIES OF THE FIELD
(1963) He won a breakthrough Oscar for his subtly witty turn as a worker building a chapel in the desert for a group of German nuns.

GUESS WHO'S COMING TO DINNER?
(1967) It now looks like a parody of earnest '60s liberalism, but Poitier plays his black suitor as a person instead of a debate position.

IN THE HEAT OF THE NIGHT
(1967) A gratifyingly commercial role as a city homicide detective teaming with a white redneck cop (Rod Steiger) in the South.

TO SIR, WITH LOVE
(1967) Coming full circle from his 'Blackboard Jungle' days, Poitier is a coolly caring teacher to an unruly British classroom.

Tom Cruise

BECAUSE THEY SEEM incapable of expressing doubt, certain stars need rescuing from the derision of critics and the people who write film histories. John Wayne was one such star. Tom Cruise is another. He has proved time and again that he can act just fine—as a callow pool shark in 'The Color of Money' (1986), as a paraplegic Vietnam vet in 'Born on the Fourth of July' (1989). Still, he is dismissed as a lightweight. Alone among his peers, Cruise has specialized in uncompli-cated valor—he's both the hero and the embodiment of 'The Firm' (1993). That Cruise has performed a number of real-life rescues makes his commitment to der-ring-do seem all the more complete. It's as if there is no longer any difference between the movies and real-ity: It's all one big 'Mission: Impossible.'

But scrape away the facade and there is still, some-where in there, Tommy Mapother, the kid brother from a broken home who played Nathan Detroit in a high school production of 'Guys and Dolls' and vowed to become a star. He joined the other Brat Pack boys in 'The Outsiders' (1983), got lucky with the same year's 'Risky Business,' and even luckier with 1986's 'Top Gun.' That role was as thin as the movie's poster. It didn't mat-ter. In 'Color of Money' and 1988's 'Rain Man,' Cruise went up against two screen titans, and both Paul New-man and Dustin Hoffman later professed themselves fans. Yet still he gets no respect. It may not matter. Cruise believes in himself, and that seems to be enough for the millions of moviegoers who flock to his certain-ty. Perhaps, someday, Cruise will be the actor to play Don Quixote, tilting at windmills and convincing even the critics that he is running at dragons. —TB

FOR ALL THE FANFARE generated by brassier talents like Spike Lee, it's sometimes hard to recall the revo-lutionary impact of the quietly powerful Poitier. He was a standout in such early films as 1955's 'The Blackboard Jungle,' but it was his Oscar-nominated turn as an escaped convict in 1958's 'The Defiant Ones' that secured his status as leading man. Thanks to Poitier 'black' and 'hero' were no longer mutually exclusive terms, and his films helped usher Americans into a new age of liberal consciousness. After winning a Best Actor Oscar in 1963 for 'Lilies of the Field,' he swiftly became a top box office draw, scoring a neat hat trick in 1967 with the hits 'Guess Who's Coming to Dinner?,' 'To Sir With Love,' and 'In the Heat of the Night.' With his ramrod dignity and ice-smooth charm, Poitier changed forever how Hollywood viewed the African-American man. (Photograph by Joel Landau) —NH

Sidney Poitier

William
Holden

HE WASN'T DASHING or matinee-idol handsome, but he became an instant star as the boxer/violinist of 'Golden Boy' (1939). After serving in WWII, Holden earned his keep as Hollywood's No. 1 regular-guy lead. With workmanlike zeal, Holden landed ripe parts in what now seems like a roster of the 1950s' greatest hits—'Sunset Boulevard,' 'Stalag 17' (for which he won a Best Actor Oscar), 'Sabrina,' 'The Bridge on the River Kwai'—and he did it all with understated style. Billy Wilder called him "the best actor of his generation," but after 40 years in film, Holden saw acting as just a job. "For me," he once said, "acting is not an all-consuming thing, except for the moment when I am actually doing it." (Photograph by Sharland)—David Hochman

"He's half child and half adult,
half innocent and half
sexual, half male and half female"
NORA EPHRON on Travolta

AS THE SWEATHOG, the Dancing Fool, and the Urban Cowboy, Travolta was the boy in the bubble of the late 1970s: a perfect, polyestered representation of sexual attitudes and outer-borough grace. He was so good at the zeitgeist gig, in fact, that it wasn't until his back-from-the-dead comeback in 1994's 'Pulp Fiction' and 1995's 'Get Shorty' that we realized what a skilled actor he was and had always been—the rather snotty assumption being that no one could fake inarticulate blue-collar smolder without actually being a lug. But Travolta is a trouper—exactly how many comebacks does this make now?—and his delightful, unexpected consistency puts him in the company of the old studio-system greats. (Photograph by Albert Watson) —TB

John
Travolta

ESSENTIAL TRAVOLTA

SATURDAY NIGHT FEVER
(1977) His star-making portrayal of a cocky, insecure disco kid is still on the money.

URBAN COWBOY
(1980) Yet another sensitive lout? Yes, but it's a deft portrait of a young man outgrowing his own sullen ego.

BLOW OUT
(1981) His movie sound-effects specialist inadvertently tapes an assassination. De Palma's best movie and Travolta's darkest.

PULP FICTION
(1994) The lithe Travolta sexiness was still there in cruel/kind hitman Vincent Vega—and so was a self-aware wit that felt brand new.

GET SHORTY
(1995) Travolta defines top-of-his-game cool as a gangland debt collector who goes Hollywood.

ESSENTIAL HOLDEN

GOLDEN BOY
(1939) Costar Barbara Stanwyck fought to get him cast as the titular young boxer. That and his own charisma launched a career.

SUNSET BOULEVARD
(1950) Stunningly self-loathing as the hack writer who gets fatally entwined with Norma Desmond (Gloria Swanson).

THE BRIDGE ON THE RIVER KWAI
(1957) The clear-sighted conscience of a great war movie, Holden's Capt. Shears escapes from hell, only to plunge back in.

THE WILD BUNCH
(1969) An aging outlaw shoots his way into the end of an era in Peckinpah's harrowing revisionist Western.

NETWORK
(1976) In his last great movie, Holden looks like the last sane man in the madhouse of modern television.

ESSENTIAL BEATTY

BONNIE AND CLYDE
(1967) He was Clyde the outlaw in this daringly violent, surprisingly tender hit.

MCCABE & MRS. MILLER
(1971) Beatty had one of his most enduring roles, as the shaggy frontier entrepreneur in Robert Altman's bittersweet fable.

SHAMPOO
(1975) A '60s sexual roundelay as seen from the cynical '70s, with the star a brilliantly shallow hairdresser stud.

REDS
(1981) Beatty burned to be taken seriously, and this three-hour epic about communist John Reed raked in the acclaim and the Oscars.

BUGSY
(1991) Easily his finest latter-day performance, as the killer dandy who meets his match while swimming with Hollywood sharks.

ESSENTIAL WASHINGTON

GLORY
(1989) Washington scored a Best Supporting Actor Oscar as a cynical volunteer in the rousing, tragic Civil War drama.

MALCOLM X
(1992) Writer-director Spike Lee fielded all the predictable controversy; Washington merely played the black leader with uncommon fire and grace.

MISSISSIPPI MASALA
(1992) His most relaxed and sexy role as a down-home carpet-cleaner who falls in love with an Asian Indian immigrant (Sarita Choudhury).

PHILADELPHIA
(1993) Hanks won the Oscar, but Washington is every bit his acting equal as a homophobic lawyer who finds tolerance through justice.

DEVIL IN A BLUE DRESS
(1995) As Easy Rawlins, the hero of detective novelist Walter Mosley's whodunit series, Washington exudes cool charisma.

Warren Beatty

HE HAS ALWAYS looked slightly distracted on screen, as if pondering all those conquests that gossipmongers and Carly Simon songs have claimed for him. So maybe Beatty should be so vain—that bemused preoccupation makes him one of the most intriguing stars of his generation. A pretty-boy Clyde in the 1967 gangster groundbreaker 'Bonnie and Clyde,' a sexually insatiable hairdresser in 1975's 'Shampoo,' the writer-director-star of the sprawling, triple-Oscar magnet 'Reds' (1981), and the playboy mobster of 1991's 'Bugsy,' Beatty has made his mark for four straight decades. Still, it is as the most durable image of the Me Generation—in front of and behind the camera—that he takes his place in movie history. —TB

WASHINGTON IS HERE not because he is the rare African American to be entrusted by the industry with mainstream leading-man roles. Audiences go to his movies expecting a fierce intelligence, a cool sexuality—and nothing more. He has played history's greats—South African activist Steven Biko in 'Cry Freedom' (1987), Malcolm in 'Malcolm X' (1992)—and he won an Oscar as a runaway slave in the Civil War epic 'Glory' (1989). But his most telling roles include race without being about it: the homophobic lawyer in 'Philadelphia' (1993), the brainy submarine officer in 'Crimson Tide' (1995), and the tormented conscience of 'Courage Under Fire' (1996). He is one of the most talented movie stars working today. Period. (Photograph by Mark Hanauer) —TB

Denzel Washington

Robert Redford

THESE DAYS REDFORD is celebrated primarily as a film impresario—the force behind the hugely influential Sundance festival and the director of prestige movies like 1994's Oscar-nominated 'Quiz Show.' It would seem an awkward transition from being the juiciest beefcake of the Me Decade. But there's always been more to Redford than his sun-kissed handsomeness—a sly charm, a wary conscientiousness, and a reputation for diverse, thoughtful roles.

His route to the silver screen reflects his natural eclecticism: He was a baseball player in college and a vagabond painter in Europe before turning to acting full-time. But it took him less than a decade to graduate from small Broadway roles to his wildly successful pairing with Paul Newman in 1969's 'Butch Cassidy and the Sundance Kid.' They reteamed in 1973's 'The Sting,' but by then the torch had already been passed. Redford—displaying both romantic idealism ('The Way We Were') and moral clarity ('All the President's Men')—had bypassed Newman in box office popularity and would become the nation's No. 1 star. Perhaps his cryptic heroes were too gorgeous for his own good: He won his only Oscar not as an actor, but as a director, for 1980's 'Ordinary People.' To avoid the hazards of the picture-perfect, he has had to escape from the camera's gaze. (Photograph by Jean Pagliuso)—NH

> "I'm drawn to his strength, his classiness, his introspectiveness, and his sadness"
> BRAD PITT

KNOWING WHAT WE DO about Hudson now—that he lived his life in a stifling Hollywood closet of sham marriages and he-man publicity—alters the pleasure of his movies not a whit. Despite the beefcake absurdity of that name (he was born Roy Harold Scherer Jr.), and despite a 1948 screen test that Twentieth Century Fox used for years as an example of bad acting, Hudson was always the most shyly witty guy on the block in the '50s and '60s, whether wooing older woman Jane Wyman in 'All That Heaven Allows' (1955) or driving Doris Day into tizzies of virginal fury in the three hit farces they made together. But by at last putting a familiar, beloved face on the "gay disease" for most of middle America, Hudson ended up playing his most important role: himself. (Photograph by Sid Avery)—TB

Rock Hudson

"I told you . . .
you know
nothing
about
wickedness"
COLUMBIA
PICTURES
presents
Rita
HAYWORTH · Orson
WELLES

The Sex Goddesses

"A SEX GODDESS isn't a real living thing. She's a plastic lady." So said Raquel Welch, who should know. And yet—we beg to differ. Of the eight actresses highlighted in this chapter, only Brigitte Bardot could truly be called a "plastic lady," inasmuch as she allowed herself to be made over into an inflatable love doll for the postwar New Sexuality. The others are pulse-quickening proof that the real erogenous zone lies between our ears.

What gives a sex goddess the oomph to propel herself to legendary status is the sense that she has a past. Marlene Dietrich shades her eyelids and drags out her syllables because accumulated erotic knowledge—so vast as to seem nearly existential—has weighed her down. Jean Harlow and Sophia Loren convey a no-nonsense air of sexual play that arises out of hard times—the Depression in Harlow's case, fascist Italy for Loren. Rita Hayworth and Ava Gardner are fascinating studies in What Was Erotic during World War II and immediately after: Hayworth, the GI's dream girl, offers dewy-eyed innocence on the outside with the promise of real sin beneath, while Gardner exudes a harder allure—sex for the Cool Jazz era.

And then there's Elizabeth Taylor, whose past unfolded in public. To screen her filmography is to see a siren come into the knowledge of her own power, from the preadolescent poise of 'National Velvet' through the naive carnality of 'A Place in the Sun' to the wise earthiness of 'Butterfield 8,' at which point films became secondary to headlines. Liz was the last old-style sex goddess; by bringing the myth into the real world, she crippled it. What simple joy was left in the come-on was destroyed with Marilyn Monroe's death (see the Top Ten). Female taboo breakers now come mainly from the rock music world; the few movie temptresses, like Sharon Stone, may have brains, but their scripts rarely do. Sadly, baring just a little means less in a world where everyone bares all. —Ty Burr

Welles' last line in 1948's 'The Lady From Shanghai' reveals what Hayworth taught him about the inexorable allure of the screen siren: "Maybe I'll live so long that I'll forget her. Maybe I'll die trying."

Elizabeth Taylor

TAYLOR LAID CLAIM to stardom practically from birth, dancing for the British royal family at age 4. She hasn't lost her regal air since: At 17, she modeled a $22,000 tiara for the Jewelry Industry Council and asked, "Can I keep it?" It's precisely because La Liz assumes glamour as a divine right that we still grant her—a 65-year-old grandmother—its spellbinding munificence.

Such natural self-command explains why, after Taylor was spotted at her father's Beverly Hills art gallery at age 10, both MGM and Universal wanted to sign her. (MGM did.) She brought a startling verisimilitude to 'National Velvet' two years later—but ascended to an even higher plane when her physical maturation caught up to her worldly sense of self. Taylor's violet eyes and raven hair set a standard of beauty for the 1950s—one so luminescent that Montgomery Clift is driven to murder in 1951's 'A Place in the Sun' so he can have her. She rode out the decade on a string of hits—'Giant' (1956), 'Raintree County' (1957), 'Cat on a Hot Tin Roof' (1958), and 'Suddenly, Last Summer' (1959)—earning Oscar nominations for the last three.

But those triumphs pale before her other talent—for a prodigious love life. She plowed through four husbands in 10 years before her epochal meeting with Richard Burton on the set of 1963's 'Cleopatra.' By then, we were used to her wonderful excess—so much so that the Taylor-Burton film 'Who's Afraid of Virginia Woolf?' dared to show the negative images of their fairy-tale romance. That she won an Oscar for the role demonstrates the reach of Taylor's stardom—not only to the heights of glitz but to the depths of a raw, unheeding passion. (Photograph by Sid Avery) —Nisid Hajari

"She was the most astonishingly self-contained, pulchritudinous, remote, removed, inaccessible woman I had ever seen"
RICHARD BURTON

"SHE HAS SEX, but no particular gender," wrote Kenneth Tynan, and that sums up Dietrich's luminous ambiguity. Although her later career boasted high points like 'A Foreign Affair' (1948), it is the seven shimmering films Dietrich made with director Josef von Sternberg in the early '30s that put her in the pantheon. In 'The Blue Angel,' 'The Scarlet Empress,' 'Shanghai Express,' and others, Von Sternberg molded his star into a baroque celluloid Venus—a creature of light who mocks men, commitment, self, and, above all, the folly of romance. Critics argue how much of the achievement was her own, but the weary whiskey of her voice is proof that at least some of it was. (Photograph by Laszlo Willinger) —Ty Burr

Marlene

ESSENTIAL DIETRICH

THE BLUE ANGEL
(1930, above) A zaftig, pre-Hollywood Dietrich warbles 'Falling in Love Again' in the Von Sternberg film that made her a household name.

SHANGHAI EXPRESS
(1932) Tough to pick only one of the shimmering Dietrich-Von Sternberg Paramount confections, but this'll do. "It took more than one man to change my name to Shanghai Lily...."

DESTRY RIDES AGAIN
(1939, below) Audiences warmed to her commercial comeback in this ribald comedy-Western opposite Jimmy Stewart.

A FOREIGN AFFAIR
(1948) Singing the praises of the "black market," she's the soul of postwar European disenchantment in Billy Wilder's acrid comedy.

WITNESS FOR THE PROSECUTION
(1958) A deceptively simple role as an accused man's ex-lover in this twisty courtroom mystery.

Jean Harlow

THE TERM 'BOMBSHELL' wasn't invented for Harlow—it just seems that way. With that platinum hair, those bee-stung lips, and the impossibly arching eyebrows, she was the epitome of cosmetically stylized glamour. But Harlow's star power was fueled by the real woman underneath. Her tough, tart, wisecracking wit gave oomph to that Max Factored image, and her proverbial heart of gold (or at least brass) completed the picture. The era's leading men—Clark Gable in 'Red Dust' (1932), Jimmy Cagney in 'The Public Enemy' (1931), and Spencer Tracy in 'Libeled Lady' (1936)—all looked better with her on their arms (and in their faces). Here's what Jimmy Stewart, her costar in 1936's 'Wife vs. Secretary,' said about kissing her: "We did the scene over and over again. They were...happy days." (Photograph by George Hurrell)—MS

"A square shooter
if there ever was one"
SPENCER TRACY

IN 1947, LIFE dubbed Rita Hayworth "The Love Goddess," and the moniker stuck. But even though this long-legged redhead made her biggest impressions as the sultry seductress peeling off a pair of elbow-length gloves in 'Gilda' (1946) and as the icy femme fatale in 'The Lady From Shanghai' (1948), Hayworth had another image in mind. "I never really thought of myself as a sex symbol," she once said. "More as a comedienne who could dance." And, boy, could she dance—opposite everyone from Fred Astaire (1942's 'You Were Never Lovelier') to Gene Kelly (1944's 'Cover Girl') to Frank Sinatra (1957's 'Pal Joey'). A Love Goddess who could also cut a rug? That was a rarity. That was Rita Hayworth. —Michael Sauter

Rita Hayworth

ESSENTIAL HAYWORTH

YOU WERE NEVER LOVELIER
(1942) That title may be right. Hayworth and Astaire dance in a dreamy Hollywood Buenos Aires.

COVER GIRL
(1944) Here she's hoofing with Gene Kelly to wonderful Kern-Gershwin songs. The whole movie's a GI's idea of heaven.

GILDA
(1946) One of the great kinky love stories in the movies, with Rita crooning "Put the Blame on Mame" while George Macready and Glenn Ford put the moves on her.

THE LADY FROM SHANGHAI
(1948) Orson Welles' scalding kiss-off to his wife: He cut off Hayworth's hair, dyed it blond, and cast her as an alluring viper.

SEPARATE TABLES
(1958) One of her finest no singing, no-dancing acting jobs, as a world-weary woman trying to rekindle a spark with Burt Lancaster.

ESSENTIAL HARLOW

PLATINUM BLONDE
(1931) This Capra treat is as stodgy as an early talkie can be, but a ripely nasal Harlow cuts through the static.

RED DUST
(1932) Can ballsy Harlow swipe man's man Gable back from ladylike Mary Astor? Say, who d'ya think yer kiddin'?

BOMBSHELL
(1933) The movie industry gets raked over the coals in a fast-paced farce that casts Harlow as a star with her head on straight.

DINNER AT EIGHT
(1933) An all-star MGM classic, with Harlow taking on a fancy dinner-party milieu with sass.

LIBELED LADY
(1936) One of the great unsung screwball comedies, with the star going into conniptions when boyfriend Spencer Tracy keeps postponing their wedding.

ESSENTIAL BARDOT

AND GOD CREATED WOMAN
(1956, below) Director Roger Vadim created the Bardot sex-kitten mythos with this shallow but sultry St. Tropez romp.

THE TRUTH
(1960) Her finest actual performance, as a headstrong runaway who falls in with Parisian intellectuals and winds up on trial for murder.

CONTEMPT
(1963) The Bardot legend gets turned on its gorgeous head in Jean-Luc Godard's condemnation of modern moviemaking. It's doubtful she got the joke.

ESSENTIAL STONE

TOTAL RECALL
(1990) After years of damsel-in-distress parts, Sharon got to display her hard-as-stone allure as Schwarzenegger's duplicitous wife.

BASIC INSTINCT
(1992) A cheesy role, sure, and based more in male fears than reality. But Stone dove so deeply into the badness that she hooked up with the zeitgeist.

CASINO
(1995) Going for the acting gold and almost getting it, Stone finally turned critics into fans as De Niro's floozy wife.

LAST DANCE
(1996) A very honorable turn as a death-row slattern, and one that might not have been overlooked if 'Dead Man Walking' hadn't stolen its thunder.

Sharon
Stone

"She's smart, which
is more than you can say
for most people who
get photographed with
some of their clothes off"
BARRY DILLER

HAS SHARON STONE made many good movies since she became a box office force in 1992's 'Basic Instinct'? Hard to argue in the face of celluloid dogs like 'Sliver' (1993) and 'Diabolique' (1996). Is she a movie star? Absolutely. In fact (and if you'll forgive our getting pointy-headed for a moment), Stone is a genuine meta-star: A Jean Harlow with added irony, she commandeers gowns and Harry Winston jewelry and carries the torch of movie glamour with witty, self-aware verve. She's a star, in other words, because she says she is. If her lack of panties in 'Instinct' vaulted her into the public eye, it's her lack of apologies—toward propriety, critics, and a male-dominated film industry—that has kept her there. (Photograph by Isabel Snyder) —TB

Brigitte
Bardot

"SEX KITTEN" IS too trivial a designation for Bardot, too suggestive of pneumatic soap stars and tabloid heroines. The French actress claims an influence far more pivotal: In 1957, 'And God Created Woman,' directed by then husband Roger Vadim, introduced her as a uniquely postwar European nymphet—freed of austerity, casually exposed, embracing an unabashed sensuality. The film won unprecedented international celebrity for Bardot; here in the U.S., her popularity almost singlehandedly pushed foreign films from the art house into the movie palace. With the country on the verge of a sexual revolution, her subsequent salacious films (and an equally juicy private life) stood at a crossroads—halfway between breathy glamour and panting lust. (Photograph by Peter Basch) —NH

Ava
Gardner

AVA GARDNER DEFINED a new sexuality for post-WWII America: As elegant as a martini glass, she was frank and impulsive, yet coolly jaded as well. She also had a beauty to make famous men swoon: Her husbands included Mickey Rooney, bandleader Artie Shaw, and Frank Sinatra (in a way, she personifies the smoky feminine ideal of the Chairman's great '50s albums). Underneath the glamorous poise, though, was a talent underrated even by herself. To Joseph Mankiewicz, who directed her as a gypsy–turned–Hollywood star in 1954's 'The Barefoot Contessa,' she said, "Hell, Joe, I'm not an actress, but I think I understand this girl. She's a lot like me." As if that isn't what acting is all about. (Photograph by Robert Capa)—TB

"She should have been sculpted in chocolate truffles so that the world could devour her" NOEL COWARD on Loren

LIFTED FROM A hardscrabble childhood and groomed by Italian producer (and eventual husband) Carlo Ponti, Loren graduated to international bombshell on the basis of a peasant sexuality—an earthy voluptuousness that hooked male admirers on both sides of the Atlantic. More unusually, her sympathetic air and evident mischievousness won her female fans as well. Even in the Hollywood films that fixated on her ample Neapolitan charms, Loren could signal a winking awareness that made her even more attractive. Her better European films, such as 1964's 'Marriage Italian Style' with Marcello Mastroianni, only cement the point—that Loren is one of the few sex symbols whose wit is as exquisite as her sultriness. (Photograph by Alfred Eisenstaedt)—NH

Sophia
Loren

THE APPEAL OF the tough guy in movies is simple, and really, it rests with the screenwriter rather than the actor. Every day we retreat from confrontations with other people, but it is the on-screen tough guy who says what we shoulda said, or coulda said, or woulda said, if only we had had the nerve or the wit or the brawn. In a world where dignity is a much-battered thing, he lets us keep ours by sharing in his refusal to back down.

It wouldn't work if he were a golden-boy hero, with no trace of sweat on his brow. But the tough guys celebrated here all have the funk of the street to them, and so their chutzpah seems within our reach. Cagney,

The Tough Guys

In 1935's 'G-Men,' James Cagney personified the movie tough guy: His New York slum kid goes gunning for gangsters after they shoot his best friend—and when the hoodlums take his girlfriend hostage, well, then Cagney really gets nasty!

Sinatra, and Pacino all rose out of very specific New York milieus; they seethe like men jostled on the subway. Robert Mitchum had done time on a Georgia chain gang; by the time he became a star, he embodied the lazy, screw-you allure of the post-WWII West Coast male. Burt Lancaster had worked as a circus acrobat, a job that gave a startling precision to his aggressiveness.

Bogart is missing from this list, of course, but he so embodied and defined the type that he's over In the Top Ten chapter—in the top spot, no less. He's so influential that every tough guy who has strolled watchfully across the screen in the past four decades owes most, if not all, of his mannerisms to Bogie. The great exception is Clint Eastwood, who cross-fertilized the urban-thriller and Western genres to give birth to a tough guy for our nihilistic times. As anyone knows who's seen Bogart and Cagney wearing cowboy hats in the misbegotten 'The Oklahoma Kid,' even the old guard couldn't pull that one off. —Ty Burr

ESSENTIAL MITCHUM

OUT OF THE PAST
(1947) He tangles sexily with Jane Greer, one of the great, tawdry B-movie femmes fatales, in one of the twistiest noirs ever.

THE LUSTY MEN
(1952) He embodies danger, poise, cynicism, and tenderness as a rodeo rider drawn to married Susan Hayward.

THE NIGHT OF THE HUNTER
(1955) His killer preacher in Charles Laughton's eerie fable remains an essential movie villain.

CAPE FEAR
(1962, above) The violence that's always lurking under a Mitchum performance finally pops out—too bad for Gregory Peck and family.

FAREWELL MY LOVELY
(1975) Long after Hollywood and Mitchum stopped making straight detective films came this graceful Philip Marlowe thriller.

Robert

Mitchum

THE RAP ON Mitchum sounds just like the praise: The
heavy-lidded eyes and sluggish drawl that many have mis-
taken for listlessness have also been celebrated as the
marks of a classically laconic, rugged persona. He turned
his sardonic manner to advantage with the onset of postwar naturalism. His performances as fatalistic shady types
in B movies like 'Out of the Past' (1947) and 'The Big
Steal' (1949)—not to mention a 1948 drug conviction—
solidified his status as a rebellious young buck; his turn
in 'The Night of the Hunter' (1955) grabbed us by the
throat. Mitchum's deadpan toughness may now look like
a stance too cool for its own time—but when it counted, he
wore it better than anyone else in Hollywood.   Nisid Hajari

James
Cagney

IF AMERICA HAS an id, it probably looks a lot like Jimmy Cagney. His restless, hair-trigger charisma conveyed charm and malice in equal measure, and the thrill of a Cagney performance lies in not knowing whether he'll reach for the girl or the grapefruit. Yes, he was a marvelous rough-neck Bottom in 'A Midsummer Night's Dream' (1935) and won an Oscar for 'Yankee Doodle Dandy' (1942), playing song-and-dance man George M. Cohan as a merry, patriotic windup toy. And in private, this former New York City slum kid was one of the truly decent men in the business. But Cagney's most unnerving roles were always his rat-a-tat gangsters, from his 'Public Enemy' breakthrough in 1931 all the way to 1949's insane 'White Heat,' in which he finally, literally, explodes. —TB

DIVORCE YOUR LOVED WITH DIGNITY

MIGUEL SANTOS
ATTORNEY

ONE

Frank
Sinatra

THE CHAIRMAN OF the Board is now such a myth that we sometimes forget he was a thespian of the first rank. We also forget that in 1952 many people thought his career was over: The vocal cords that had once caused so many million young girls to swoon had hemorrhaged, and Hollywood no longer wanted him. Then along came the role of Pvt. Angelo Maggio in 'From Here to Eternity' (1953), a part Sinatra wanted and accepted for a humiliating $8,000. His gamble paid off: He won a Best Supporting Actor Oscar; two years later, in 1955, he was nominated in the Best Actor category for playing the junkie drummer in 'The Man With the Golden Arm.' Maybe if he had gotten two other parts he wanted—lead roles in 'On the Waterfront' and 'Dirty Harry'—Sinatra the actor would have been more in tune with Sinatra the singer. (Photograph by Bob Willoughby)—Steve Wulf

"The blue eyes were inquisitive, the smile bright and audacious" AVA GARDNER

HE CAME ON like Dustin Hoffman's sexy kid brother: brooding, volcanic, the most mesmerizing fusion of Method acting and charisma since the young Brando. As with Robert De Niro, the pleasure of Pacino's performances is in waiting for that moment when he finally pops his cork—"Attica! Attica!"—but the scenes leading up to the explosions offer riches of their own. A movie MIA during much of the '80s, Pacino returned in the '90s to acclaim, one more shot at Michael Corleone (they kept pulling him back in), and an Oscar for 1992's 'Scent of a Woman.' His current mannered hamminess, however enjoyable, can't touch the incandescence of his early-'70s work: 'Serpico,' 'Dog Day Afternoon,' and above all, the first two 'Godfathers,' in which he becomes an emblem of all-American rot. (Photograph by Sante D'Orazio) —TB

Al
Pacino

Spencer Tracy

IN 1926, PRODUCER George M. Cohan closed the dress rehearsal for one of his plays by telling a 26-year-old actor from Milwaukee, "Spencer Tracy, you're the best damn actor I ever saw." This, mind you, was before Tracy had made any of his 73 movies or received one of his nine Academy Award nominations. He wasn't much of a looker, with his granite face and square build. But he was so natural and commanding that he elevated character acting to top billing. The winner of consecutive Best Actor Oscars for 'Captains Courageous' (1937) and 'Boys Town' (1938), Tracy could alternately charm, inspire, and challenge audiences. His own secret of success, he said, was simple: "Just know your lines and don't bump into the furniture." In 1942's 'Woman of the Year,' he began a court-and-spark relationship with Katharine Hepburn that produced nine movies—including 1948's 'State of the Union,' 1949's 'Adam's Rib,' and 1952's 'Pat and Mike'—and lasted the rest of his life. He had his own demons, alcohol being one of them, but whether Tracy was playing a simple fisherman or Father Flanagan or Dr. Jekyll and Mr. Hyde, he projected, in the words of Sir Laurence Olivier, "great truth." As it turned out, George M. Cohan was right. (Photograph by J.R. Eyerman) —SW

> "He is an actor's star. He is a people's star. His quality is clear and direct. Ask a question—get an answer. No pause."
> **KATHARINE HEPBURN**
> on Tracy

A GENTLE, LITERATE soul with the face of a catfish and a voice like a sour trombone, Robinson was a leading man caught in a character actor's body. Born Emmanuel Goldenberg in Bucharest, Romania, he adopted America, then a new name (the 'G,' he said later, stood for "God only knows or gangsters"), then the Broadway stage, and finally Hollywood. It was the brute immigrant swagger of gangster Rico Bandello (read: Al Capone) in 1931's 'Little Caesar' that made Robinson's name, but it was the actor's skill and humanity that marked his finest roles, especially the well-meaning but doomed heroes of Fritz Lang's 'The Woman in the Window' (1944) and 'Scarlet Street' (1945). Still, it's for his impatient villainy in films like 'Caesar' and 'Key Largo' (1948) that he's enshrined in the repertoire of cocktail-party impressionists everywhere. Nyahhh, see? —TB

Edward G. Robinson

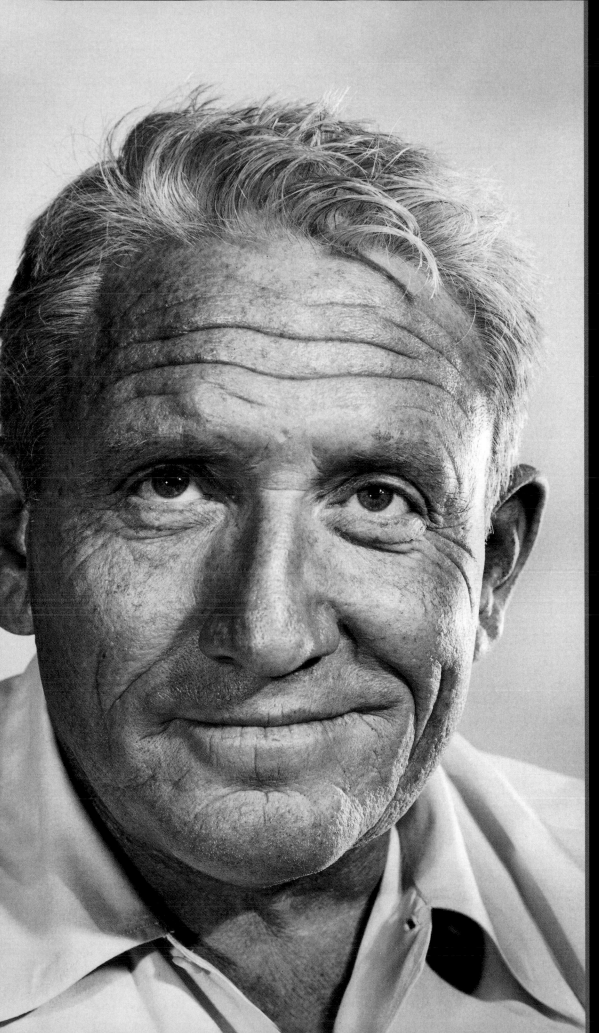

ESSENTIAL ROBINSON

LITTLE CAESAR
(1931) Cagney was the gangster as charming killer; Robinson made his name, by contrast, as a graceless, unstoppable runt.

DOUBLE INDEMNITY
(1944) A supporting role, yes—but he's the movie's avuncular conscience as a suspicious claims investigator.

THE WOMAN IN THE WINDOW
(1944) Robinson is cast way against type as a well intentioned lovelorn sucker in Fritz Lang's bitter thriller.

SCARLET STREET
(1945) His second for Lang is a devastating tale of a middle-class weekend painter who finds a ruinous muse in tarty Joan Bennett.

KEY LARGO
(1948) A triumphantly squalid return to out-and-out villainy, puffing on a stogie in the bathtub as hero Bogie tries to smoke him out.

ESSENTIAL TRACY

FURY
(1936) Tracy smolders as the vengeance-minded victim of a lynch mob in Fritz Lang's cauterizing drama.

CAPTAINS COURAGEOUS
(1937) He won his first Oscar for a sentimental, yet honestly tough, portrayal of a Portuguese fisherman befriended by a rich boy.

BOYS TOWN
(1938) Tracy went Oscar two for two by playing Father Flanagan, the hardheaded, softhearted founder of the home for troubled kids.

ADAM'S RIB
(1949) The archetypal Tracy-Hepburn comedy sets the two at legal loggerheads as married attorneys on opposite sides of a case.

FATHER OF THE BRIDE
(1950) This disarming suburban comedy gave Tracy one of his most affable latter-day roles—a far cry from the fury of 'Fury.'

ESSENTIAL LANCASTER

THE KILLERS
(1946) A brawny, sensitive debut in a rock-solid film noir based on a Hemingway story.

SWEET SMELL OF SUCCESS
(1957) In Lancaster's hands, powerful gossip columnist J. J. Hunsecker becomes a paradigm of modern-day evil.

ELMER GANTRY
(1960) He won an Oscar for his bogus Bible-thumper, talking from both sides of his mouth and all the more alluring for it.

BIRDMAN OF ALCATRAZ
(1962) A precise, stark, true story of a prison lifer who, from his cell, becomes an authority on birds.

ATLANTIC CITY
(1981) A low-level Mob runner suddenly has a chance to get it all: the girl, the money, respect. It's Lancaster's last great shot, too.

ESSENTIAL EASTWOOD

THE GOOD, THE BAD, AND THE UGLY
(1966) The best of the Leone-Eastwood pasta oaters: a violent epic comedy about greed and retribution.

DIRTY HARRY
(1971) Like its star, this modern policier is far more complex than its reputation—but just as brutally no-nonsense.

PLAY MISTY FOR ME
(1971) 'Fatal Attraction' 16 years early, this scary directorial debut proved he was smarter than his screen image suggested.

UNFORGIVEN
(1992) In a rich meditation on heroes, the quiet, deadly cowboy of the spaghetti Westerns gets updated with grave misgivings.

THE BRIDGES OF MADISON COUNTY
(1995) Who could possibly have guessed that Clint would turn the drippy best-seller into a surpassingly touching romance—and show his soft side in the bargain?

Burt Lancaster

LIKE HIS FREQUENT costar Kirk Douglas, Lancaster parlayed good luck and athleticism into a career that lasted, well, from here to eternity. Although he didn't appear in his first movie until he was 32, as Swede in 'The Killers' (1946), Lancaster quickly established himself as an action hero. And when he saw action on the beach with Deborah Kerr in 'From Here to Eternity' (1953), he became one of Hollywood's biggest stars. Lancaster had more depth and staying power than Hollywood first imagined, winning an Oscar for 'Elmer Gantry' (1960) and earning nods for 'Birdman of Alcatraz' (1962) and 'Atlantic City' (1981). One of his last roles with Douglas was in 1981's 'The Boys in Autumn,' a play about the final days of Tom Sawyer and Huck Finn. Lancaster was—and always will be—Huck. —SW

> "Eastwood is a man who works in the American vernacular, an artisan whose art emerges from his craft" RICHARD SCHICKEL, critic

Clint Eastwood

EASTWOOD'S IMPORTANCE, initially, was as a John Wayne for an age without innocence. His spaghetti-Western cowboys were Wayne heroes who defended widows and children only if there was money to be made, and 'Dirty Harry' imagined a John Wayne shooting the bad guys and to hell with due process. All of which made Eastwood, during the 1970s, a no-brow bugaboo for liberals and beady-eyed idol for the right.

But a funny thing happened over the next two decades: He slowly gained in stature as a thinking man, as an actor of terse skill, as a director of taste and commercial daring. In 1993, Eastwood won Oscars for producing and directing the tough, wounded anti-Western 'Unforgiven,' and everyone from critics to the man in the street thought justice had been served. Even his fans in 1967 would have found such a notion mind-boggling.

The weirdest part is that Clint hasn't changed much in his 30-year career. We, instead, have come to him. It's true he has chosen to show more of himself over the years: the jazz freak of 'Bird' (1988), the redneck raconteur of the orangutan comedies, a prober of macho moral doubt in 'Tightrope' (1984) and 'In the Line of Fire' (1993). But the basic Clint squint remains the same—it's just that we now ascribe wit to it.

There is little that is humorous in 'Unforgiven,' but the film's gaze is astoundingly democratic—not only is it the rare movie totally without "good guys" and "bad guys," it goes so far as to address the very absurdity of such concepts. As great a pop provocateur as when he started, Clint Eastwood has stuck to his guns. (Photograph by Bill Eppridge) —TB

The Beauties

MORE THAN ANY other medium, the movies are a hothouse for female beauty. The camera can bring us much closer than the theater, with phalanxes of makeup artists, hairdressers, and couturiers smoothing over the pesky physical flaws that such nearness reveals. The movies, too, capture the ideal for eternity: We will always have Garbo staring over the bow of the ship at the end of 'Queen Christina.' The attached curse is that we will also always have, say, a distressingly aged Veronica Lake at the tail end of her career, ranting away in 'Flesh Feast.' For all the world-weary knowledge she displayed in her roles, Garbo's greatest wisdom may have been to close up shop at age 36, her looks still intact, and run from the cameras.

The close-up could have been invented for Garbo, aglow in this poster for 1930's 'Anna Christie.' The care lavished on her by MGM's cameramen would later influence the way other beauties like Vivien Leigh and Grace Kelly were presented on screen.

And yet, the women in this chapter are not here merely for their beauty. In many cases—Michelle Pfeiffer being perhaps the best example—they have had to actually overcome their looks, and the suspicion of shallowness that goes hand in hand with it, before being taken seriously as actresses. The face is a token, yes, but it's what lies behind the face that lasts.

Take Audrey Hepburn, who so stunned moviegoers in her first lead role, in 1953's 'Roman Holiday,' that she won a Best Actress Oscar and, 23 years later, was a luminously weathered Maid Marian in 'Robin and Marian.' Or Olivia de Havilland, who, when she wasn't being shunted into ladylike parts, could find the spiritual beauty in the most put-upon heroines. Or, more recently, Julia Roberts, who shimmered with grinning ease in 'Pretty Woman' and whose subsequent refusal, or inability, to consistently rebottle that magic is willful, brave, and maddening. We pay to see these women because they are lovely—and to experience an inner radiance that finds its form in outward grace. —Ty Burr

Audrey Hepburn

"Is there a woman who would not want to look like Audrey?" HUBERT DE GIVENCHY

ESSENTIAL HEPBURN

ROMAN HOLIDAY
(1953) She burst upon the scene in her first leading role as a princess on the run—and a charmed Hollywood gave her an Oscar.

FUNNY FACE
(1957) Young Hepburn and aging Astaire: It's a bad match only on paper. Both are so otherworldly they make this musical a smart treat.

BREAKFAST AT TIFFANY'S
(1961, above) So it dilutes the Truman Capote original: Hepburn is heartbreakingly carefree as Gotham gal Holly Golightly.

MY FAIR LADY
(1964) Taking the role that Julie Andrews originated on stage and making it her own. Loverly indeed.

ROBIN AND MARIAN
(1976) A middle-aged Robin Hood (Sean Connery) renews love with his grave, graceful Maid. One of the wisest romances ever filmed.

SHE CONSIDERED HERSELF funny-looking, which just goes to show that beauty really is in the eye of the beholder. For when the rest of the world watched Hepburn, it beheld beauty of a most singular kind. Her gamine glamour stood out in fresh contrast to the voluptuous images of fellow '50s stars like Elizabeth Taylor and Marilyn Monroe. With her ballet dancer's body, radiant smile, and great dark eyes, Hepburn was a vision of girlish loveliness: graceful, guileless, lighter than air. She won an Oscar for her first starring role, as the runaway princess in 'Roman Holiday' (1953), and forever after shone brightest in such romantic comedies as 'Funny Face' (1957) and 'Breakfast at Tiffany's' (1961). Her Sabrina was irresistible, her Holly Golightly enchanting. Though she downplayed the skill it took to embody these ladies, there was no denying the depth she brought to her roles as the conflicted woman of God in 'The Nun's Story' (1959); as Albert Finney's wife in the bittersweet marital odyssey 'Two for the Road' (1967); as the aging Maid Marian in the autumnal 'Robin and Marian' (1976). The bloom of her beauty barely faded over the years (she gave her last performance, as an angel, in 1989's 'Always'), and the actress that was Hepburn continued to blossom—slowly, surely, sublimely. (Photograph by Dennis Stock)—Michael Sauter

Greta

AS GREAT AN ENIGMA as she was in her movies, she was an even greater one off screen. Garbo came to Hollywood from Sweden in 1925 and quickly became a sensation in silent melodramas. It was sound, though, that deepened her persona: Her voice ached with regret even as her characters immolated themselves in romance all the more delicious for being doomed. 'Queen Christina' (1933) and 'Camille' (1937) are the two that live up to the legend; so does the 50-year seclusion she went into after 'Two-Faced Woman' (1941). Katharine Hepburn called her "a mysterious sailboat who disappeared over the horizon the moment she felt she couldn't cope." Even after death, she's the sphinx of Hollywood, a ghostly rebuke to the whole notion of stardom. (Photograph by George Hurrell)—TB

ESSENTIAL PFEIFFER

INTO THE NIGHT
(1985) Pfeiffer rings deft changes on the stock femme-fatale role as she leads schmo Jeff Goldblum into danger.

DANGEROUS LIAISONS
(1988) Going the acting distance and picking up a Best Supporting Actress nomination as a virtuous woman betrayed by love.

MARRIED TO THE MOB
(1988) As a Mafia widow trying to leave the Mob behind, she comes off like Carole Lombard's shier sister.

THE FABULOUS BAKER BOYS
(1989) Watching Pfeiffer sing "Makin' Whoopee" as she crawls on a piano is a major movie moment.

BATMAN RETURNS
(1992, above) Her transformation from much-abused secretary to latex-swathed mistress of kink is both comic and scarily on the money.

ESSENTIAL LEIGH

GONE WITH THE WIND
(1939) How she came from nowhere to nail one of the most-coveted roles in years is one of the great Hollywood myths. And it's all true.

WATERLOO BRIDGE
(1940) A creamy, passionate romance set in wartime London—love under the Luftwaffe—between Leigh and Robert Taylor.

THAT HAMILTON WOMAN
(1941) The tabloid scandal of the 18th century, with Olivier a dashing Lord Nelson and real-life paramour Leigh as dazzling Lady Hamilton.

A STREETCAR NAMED DESIRE
(1951) A refined, deluded Blanche Du Bois, cracking under the torments of modernity and Brando.

Vivien Leigh

AS SCARLETT O'HARA in 1939's 'Gone With the Wind,' Leigh was spunky, spiteful, headstrong, and heroic. Even if she'd never appeared on screen again, that one Oscar-winning performance would have made her a Hollywood legend. But Mrs. Laurence Olivier didn't stop there. Starring opposite her celebrated husband, she carried herself like a queen in 1941's 'That Hamilton Woman' (Winston Churchill's favorite film). A decade later, she clashed epically with Marlon Brando—and won her second Oscar—as the definitive Blanche Du Bois in 'A Streetcar Named Desire.' Her too-short career was interrupted by myriad illnesses, but this breathtaking beauty did nothing small—and she did it all exquisitely. (Photograph by Laszlo Willinger)—MS

Michelle Pfeiffer

FEW ACTRESSES of her generation have had to swim upstream quite so hard. The way Hollywood sees things, there are Babes and there are Actresses, and Pfeiffer was such a Babe for the first part of her career that her gossamer loveliness condemned her as an ornament in the eyes of critics and audiences alike. Nor did it help that her first major role was in the woebegone 'Grease 2'; in 1982, her star wattage couldn't compare with the blinding charisma of, um, Olivia Newton-John. But with 1985's 'Into the Night,' Pfeiffer began to show a flair for wounded comedy; and with her stunning, nervy dramatic performances at the turn of the decade—'Dangerous Liaisons,' 'The Fabulous Baker Boys,' 'The Russia House'—even a churl or a studio executive had to recognize her gift. (Photograph by Peggy Sirota)—TB

> "You couldn't really say Michelle is glacial, but there's obviously something oscillating below the surface there"
> JACK NICHOLSON on Pfeiffer

Grace Kelly

LIKE THE FIREWORKS that provide the backdrop to her love scene with Cary Grant in 'To Catch a Thief' (1955), Grace Kelly was both incandescent and evanescent. The Philadelphia socialite first caught our eyes in 'High Noon' (1952). She won the 1954 Best Actress Oscar, ostensibly for 'The Country Girl,' but also in recognition of her amazing run that year: 'Dial M for Murder,' 'Rear Window,' and 'Green Fire.' Before she became a princess, Kelly had a serene highness—and a wink of passion that made her unbearably sexy. (It never made sense that Jimmy Stewart would look out that window when he could look at her.) When Kelly wed Monaco's Prince Rainier in 1956, ending her film career, millions of hearts were broken.—Steve Wulf

SHE WAS THE ESSENCE of outlaw cool as the bank-robbing Bonnie Parker in 1967's 'Bonnie and Clyde,' her slinky mid-calf skirts and cockeyed berets inspiring a wave of retro-'30s fashion. But while she found her early fame as a poster girl for young, hip Hollywood, Dunaway was really a throwback: an actress loaded with golden-age glamour in an era of blue jeans. Chic and alluring in films like 1974's 'Chinatown' and 1976's 'Network' (for which she won a Best Actress Oscar), she inspired comparisons to both the cool beauty of Grace Kelly and the mystery of Greta Garbo. It seems inevitable she'd take on the larger-than-life role of Joan Crawford in 1981's chilling 'Mommie Dearest.' After all, she knew what being a legend was all about. (Photograph by Michael Tighe) —MS

Faye Dunaway

ESSENTIAL DE HAVILLAND

A MIDSUMMER NIGHT'S DREAM
(1935) Only 19 years old, she debuted as a delightfully high-spirited Hermia in this daft Hollywood Shakespeare.

GONE WITH THE WIND
(1939) Saintly Melanie suffers and suffers—but Scarlett gets all the best lines. Still, it established De Havilland as a serious dramatic actress.

TO EACH HIS OWN
(1946) Her first Oscar, for playing a martyred mom in one of the great women's weepies (we defy you not to lose it at the end).

THE SNAKE PIT
(1948) Shredding her ladylike image with a harrowing portrait of a mental patient.

THE HEIRESS
(1949) De Havilland's playing of a woman seduced and scorned in 19th-century New York won her a second Oscar.

ESSENTIAL ROBERTS

MYSTIC PIZZA
(1988) The calm before the storm: Roberts is rawly radiant as a small-town beauty stuck behind the pizza counter.

STEEL MAGNOLIAS
(1989) Holding her own (the death scene helped) among serious competition: Sally Field, Dolly Parton, Shirley MacLaine, to name a few.

PRETTY WOMAN
(1990) Roberts' infectious, googly grace brought warmth to a far-fetched fairy tale. Okay, so 'Breakfast at Tiffany's' was about a call girl too.

SOMETHING TO TALK ABOUT
(1995) After countless clanky Hollywood contraptions had dimmed her allure, she sprang back in this low-key but biting comedy.

MY BEST FRIEND'S WEDDING
(1997) Radiant once more in a screwball revenge farce that brought the pretty woman back into the spotlight.

Olivia
de Havilland

SHE EMBODIED a screen persona so gracious, kind, and unwimpy that a whole school of lesser gentlewomen—Greer Garson, Deborah Kerr, et al.—grew up in her wake. De Havilland rarely played upper-class doyennes, although she won her second Best Actress Oscar as the plain-Jamesian heroine of 'The Heiress' (1949) and was a lovely Maid Marian in 'The Adventures of Robin Hood' (1938). Rather, her métier was middle-class nobility, especially in 'Hold Back the Dawn' (1941) and 'To Each His Own' (her first Oscar, in 1946). It is as Melanie in 'Gone With the Wind' (1939) that we know her best, though, and the fact that De Havilland made us like someone so good when we had Scarlett to love is proof of her self-effacing gifts. —TB

"Men think Julia is extraordinarily beautiful. And women think they went to school with her." SALLY FIELD

JULIA ROBERTS' daft, misshapen career illustrates the benign tyranny that can ensue when moviegoers fall in love en masse. With 'Pretty Woman' (1990), she was embraced by audiences as an Audrey Hepburn for the naughty '90s, a girl glowing with off-kilter glamour. Yet nothing Roberts has done since—on screen or off—has matched the charisma of that unrealistic confection. She first grabbed the audience's attention in 1988's 'Mystic Pizza,' followed by a heartrending performance in 1989's 'Steel Magnolias.' Against all odds, those luminous, expectant eyes continue to hold us, despite lame thrillers, tabloid rumors, surprising nuptials, and all those "new Julia Robertses." It's as though we so need someone of such loosey-goosey charm that we are willing to forgive all. Astoundingly, she is only 28; her story will have many, many more chapters. (Photograph by Firooz Zahedi) —TB

Julia
Roberts

Every

guys

WHY WOULD WE go to the movies if not for the actors in this chapter? The stars would seem so godlike, so unapproachable; in a world of Cary Grants, we would all feel like Ralph Bellamy. But there are performers who can fit into leading-man roles, or play tough guys and action heroes, yet transcend stereotypes and speak to our own dreams. They're the Joes: stars who seem enough like us to make what happens in movies seem possible, yet with enough rough edges sanded off to make a difference.

They are the most American figures in this most American of mediums, democratic in a way that the heroes of 19th-century European literature could never

have been. It's no coincidence that any one of these guys would fit right into a film about the Revolutionary War (okay, so Michael Douglas would probably want to play Benedict Arnold). Likewise, Mark Twain would doubtless approve the casting of Henry Fonda, Harrison Ford, or Kevin Costner for any of his works (although Tom Hanks may be closer to the cynical Clemens wavelength). There is a plainspoken resilience to these actors that is entwined beyond words with the country's sense of self, so much so that an immigrant named Frank Capra could see Gary Cooper as John Doe himself.

We are lucky to have a number of stars working this turf in our generation, several of whom admittedly owe a large debt to Jimmy Stewart (see the Top Ten chapter). Costner building a ball field for ghosts, Hanks relating his life from a bus-stop bench, Ford making a Tom Clancy hero human—in an era in which we don't trust conventional leading men, it's the Everyguys who reassure us that miracles can still happen in movies and, maybe, in life. —Ty Burr

As Tom Joad in 1940's 'The Grapes of Wrath,' Fonda is the ultimate Everyguy, declaring his social resolve with an almost mystical fervor: 'Wherever there's a fight so hungry people can eat, I'll be there. Wherever there's a cop beatin' up a guy, I'll be there."

"The gentlest
man I've ever known"
AUDREY HEPBURN

Gregory Peck

WITH HIS BEST Actor Oscar for 'To Kill a Mockingbird' (1962), Peck became a noble father figure to the baby-boom generation. In truth, the beneficent, liberal small-town lawyer Atticus Finch was a kind of Hollywood stand-in for John F. Kennedy, and it is a tribute to Peck's cautious goodness that his reputation, at least, remains unsullied in the '90s. He vaulted to dreamboat stardom in the mid-'40s playing a priest in 'The Keys of the Kingdom' (1944) and an amnesiac hunk in 'Spellbound' (1945), and his gentle valor was amply displayed in 'The Yearling' (1946), 'Gentleman's Agreement' (1947), and 'Roman Holiday' (1953). But a funkier, darker Peck emerges in films like 'Duel in the Sun' (1946) and 'Twelve O'Clock High' (1949)—intriguing hints of skeletons in Atticus Finch's closet. —TB

Henry Fonda

IN AN AGE of Hollywood gods and goddesses, Fonda
made his legend by being one of us. Though he played his
share of epic characters, they always seemed life-size
coming from him. True grit and gumption ran through
all his great roles, from idealistic Tom Joad in 'The
Grapes of Wrath' (1940) to irascible old Norman Thayer
in 'On Golden Pond' (1981), the latter earning him a
Best Actor Oscar. Villains were rare for this lanky, laconic Nebraskan—quite simply, Fonda was about heroes.
Both the lone cowboy trying to stop a lynching in 'The
Ox-Bow Incident' (1943) and the U.S. President striving
to prevent a nuclear war in 'Fail-Safe' (1964) were quintessential Fonda: the American Everyman, rising to the
occasion. (Photograph by Zinn Arthur) —Michael Sauter

"He was wonderful to play with—very true—very natural"
KATHARINE HEPBURN

ESSENTIAL FONDA

THE GRAPES OF WRATH
(1940, above) As novelist John Steinbeck said after watching Fonda play Tom Joad in the dust-bowl classic, "I believed my own story again."

THE LADY EVE
(1941, below) Twice fleeced by tootsie Barbara Stanwyck in Preston Sturges' sidesplitter, Fonda plays the sympathetic boob in a delightful turn.

12 ANGRY MEN
(1957) He's the soul of liberal, thoughtful decency as the lone jury holdout on a hot, fractious day.

ONCE UPON A TIME IN THE WEST
(1968) In Sergio Leone's epic masterpiece, Fonda gets the countercasting of his life as a black-clad, incredibly mean hired killer.

ON GOLDEN POND
(1981) Calling on real-life resonances for much of its sentimental power, this graceful swan song won Fonda his only Oscar.

MR. DEEDS GOES TO TOWN
(1936, below) He's Frank
Capra's pixilated common
man, winning a fortune, a
high-comedy court case,
and Jean Arthur.

BALL OF FIRE
(1941) Beautifully out to
lunch as a poindexter
professor who sets out to
investigate modern slang and
comes home with
Barbara Stanwyck.

SERGEANT YORK
(1941) A tough role—Alvin
York was a religious pacifist
who became WWI's greatest
American hero—but Cooper
took it all the way to
the Oscars.

**THE PRIDE
OF THE YANKEES**
(1942) Even if they had to
flip the negative over to
make Coop a lefty, he's
achingly fine as doomed
Lou Gehrig.

HIGH NOON
(1952, below) He clocked his
second Academy Award as
Marshal Will Kane,
gracefully facing down bad
guys with no help
from the good.

"That guy just
represents
America for me"
FRANK CAPRA

Gary
Cooper

LIKE LOU GEHRIG, Gary Cooper considered himself the
luckiest man on the face of the earth. "I'm Mr. Average
Joe American," he once said in explaining his enduring
popularity among both men and women—from 1936 to
1957, he was consistently among Hollywood's top 10
box office draws. Cooper, a Montanan who went to
Hollywood to become a cartoonist, came to represent
the strong, silent type (1932's 'A Farewell to Arms'), but
he could also be a delightful comedian (1936's 'Mr.
Deeds Goes to Town'). That versatility helped him snare
two Oscars (for 1941's 'Sergeant York' and 1952's
'High Noon'). Still, it was hard to separate the man
from his most famous role, in 1942's 'The Pride of the
Yankees.' Once, while entertaining rain-soaked GIs in
the Pacific, Cooper complied with a request to do Gehrig's
farewell speech. When he had finished, 15,000 men were
in tears. (Photograph by Johnny Florea)—Steve Wulf

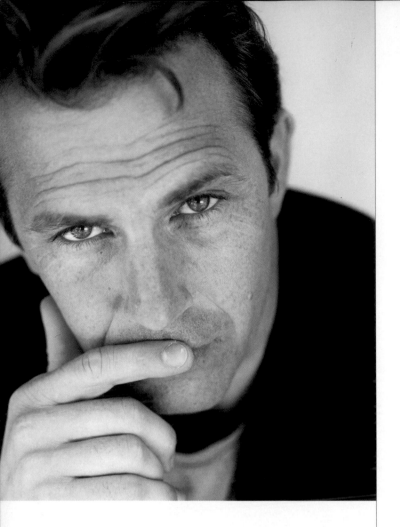

Tom Hanks

LIKE JIMMY STEWART, Tom Hanks is in imminent danger of becoming too beloved. The one-two Oscar punch of 'Philadelphia' (1993) and 'Forrest Gump' (1994), followed by the foursquare heroics of 'Apollo 13' (1995), have made him a legend almost before his time, and even Hanks seems suspicious of the acclaim.

What an odd place for the 1974 Class Cutup of Skyline High in Oakland to find himself in. Starting with Ron Howard's 'Splash' (1984), Hanks balanced doubting-Tom brassiness (which appealed to men) and rueful gentleness (which reeled in the women). If this were the '30s, Hanks would be stuck playing the hero's best friend, but these days we are reluctant to trust heroes who look too good. We do trust Tom Hanks.

'Big' (1988) put Hanks' tenderness on the block, but it was the same year's 'Punchline' that hinted at Oscars to come; as a stand-up comic with his ego in overdrive, Hanks is scarifying—you almost have to avert your eyes during his onstage nervous breakdown—and the best thing in the movie.

He found a new romantic lightness in 1993's 'Sleepless in Seattle.' Then came the holy trinity of 'Philadelphia,' 'Gump,' and 'Apollo 13,' and Hanks' apotheosis into America's dream of itself took shape. But while he deserves every accolade he gets, something is missing at the moment, and you have to catch the actor on a talk show to find it. There, there it is: the sardonic joy that fills Hanks' voice as he spins a hilarious yarn about bellhopping for Slappy White, the little verbal riffs, the outraged grumping at life's indignities. Hanks' hidden strength remains the self-mocking dexterity of the Class Cutup. It's not part of the act right now, but he's too damned smart to let it disappear for good. (Photograph by Nigel Parry)—TB

EVERY ERA has its Everyman, and ours is Costner. He first announced himself almost a decade ago in upright, vulnerable roles like the world-weary catcher "Crash" Davis in 1988's 'Bull Durham' and G-man Eliot Ness in 1987's 'The Untouchables.' With his stolid, Cooperesque manliness, he tapped into an irresistible vein of pure, all-American heroes, whether playing the idealistic, baseball-loving dad in 'Field of Dreams' (1989), the romantic title character of 'The Bodyguard' (1992), or the sensitive frontiersman in his 1990 labor of love, 'Dances With Wolves' (which earned the star two Oscars, for Best Picture and Best Director). With Costner, it hardly matters that he's not holding up a mirror: We could never be so good, which is why we find him so great. (Photograph by Diego Uchitel)—Nisid Hajari

Kevin Costner

ESSENTIAL COSTNER

THE UNTOUCHABLES
(1987) Amid the showboating star power of this De Palma hit, Costner essayed a low-key Eliot Ness—and a star was born.

BULL DURHAM
(1988) Costar Tim Robbins got the girl (Susan Sarandon) in real life, but Costner has his sexiest role as a burned-out minor league catcher.

FIELD OF DREAMS
(1989) Here's where the Cooper comparisons really started. He's an Iowa farmer who finds ghosts and redemption in this magical fable.

DANCES WITH WOLVES
(1990) He triumphed as star, director, and producer for this pointed Western epic, even if some viewers missed his raffish grin.

TIN CUP
(1996) As a stubborn, goofball, down-on-his-luck golf pro, Costner relocated his charismatic swing after too many sour dramas.

ESSENTIAL HANKS

SPLASH
(1984) At last: a fish-out-of-water story about a real fish. And in his first lead, the Tom Hanks we know and love already seems complete.

BIG
(1988) A boy finds himself in a man's body and spends a wonderful, terrible time trying to get back. This smash seemed tailored to the star's man-child talents.

PUNCHLINE
(1988) An astounding, little-seen performance, with Hanks in harrowing overdrive as a neurotic stand-up comedian.

PHILADELPHIA
(1993) His first Oscar, for playing an AIDS-afflicted lawyer, deftly and heart-breakingly showing the dilemmas of the corporate closet.

FORREST GUMP
(1994) And Oscar No. 2, for this zeitgeist hit about a deceptively simple man living through horrifically complicated times.

Michael

Harrison

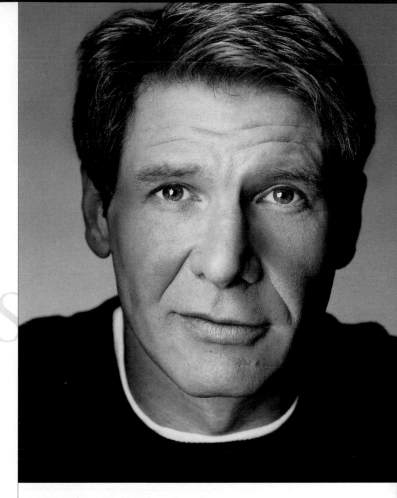

DOUGLAS HAS BEEN many things in his 30-year career— a callow TV cop, an Oscar-winning producer, a romantic lead—but middle age has finally brought him greater meaning within the pop-culture landscape. In films like 'Fatal Attraction' (1987), 'Basic Instinct' (1992), and 'Disclosure' (1994), Douglas is the epitome of the old-guard American Man thrown against the ropes by modern (read: eeevil) American Woman. As a poster boy for modern male discomfort, he has engendered rage and empathy in equal parts, but it's not often noticed how darkly Douglas plays these guys—how hornswoggled they are by their own errant hormones. He's a rare bird in Hollywood: an actor whose risk taking seems to increase with age. (Photograph by Terry O'Neill) —TB

FORD IS THE ON-SCREEN stand-in for the whiz-kid directors who invigorated Hollywood in the 1970s. For Spielberg and Lucas, in fact, he is a central figure: Both the 'Star Wars' and 'Indiana Jones' triptychs would be far shallower comic books without Ford's wonderfully hesitant derring-do. Notably, he doesn't mean much to Coppola's cosmology, despite appearing in 'The Conversation' (1974) and 'Apocalypse Now' (1979)—it may simply be that Ford's persona isn't flamboyantly flawed enough to interest Saint Francis.

Not that Ford has avoided troubled and troublesome characters. On the contrary, as he has matured on screen, he has strived for serious roles: a burned-out 21st-century private investigator in the groundbreaking 'Blade Runner' (1982), an adulterous lawyer in 'Presumed Innocent' (1990), a brain-damaged yuppie in 'Regarding Henry' (1991). His characters in love— in 1985's 'Witness' or 1988's 'Working Girl'—are quietly impassioned. Yet even when Ford tumbles into the merely glum, he retains the adoration of mass audiences—in this, too, he is like his mentor Spielberg—and his efforts are paying off with recent roles (1993's 'The Fugitive,' the two Tom Clancy films) that put his new solemnity into a fetchingly commercial context. He has kept the modesty of the carpenter he once was; he now has the grave charisma of a Fonda or a Cooper. —TB

The Artists

"IN YOUR HEART of hearts, you know perfectly well that movie stars aren't artists," said Marlon Brando in a late-'70s interview. He almost got it right. Yes, we revere many movie stars for their charisma rather than their craft. But there are craftsmen and women of such exacting rigor and mesmerizing gifts that we have no real choice but to call them movie stars, too.

Originally, the Hollywood factory had no preset mold for artistry; the actors singled out as geniuses invariably carried British accents and traces of greasepaint from playing Hamlet at the Old Vic. Case in point: Laurence Olivier, who came to Hollywood in the early '30s and was wasted in minor roles. Back he went to Olde England, and after a succession of critically lauded stage productions, he returned triumphantly as Heathcliff in 'Wuthering Heights' and as a director of daring cinematic Shakespeare. Even as late as the early '60s, a plummy Welsh accent marked brooding Richard Burton as a Serious Actor.

With the arrival of Brando (see the Top Ten chapter), Americans got their own homegrown artiste—the first movie star to tear down the walls of celebrity with all-encompassing Method. Such was the Brando revolution that all conscious screen "artists" since have worked in his shadow: Dustin Hoffman spitting in celebrity's face as Ratso Rizzo in 'Midnight Cowboy,' cerebral Meryl Streep collecting Oscar nominations like supermarket coupons, Robert De Niro raging like Marlon's crazed cousin, Jessica Lange fleeing King Kong for the higher pinnacles of craft. These are not movie stars in the classic Hollywood sense; they often make us work as hard as they themselves do. But does anyone really believe the rewards aren't worth it? —Ty Burr

"He'll put himself
out on a limb.
In fact, he'll put
himself out on
a twig of a tree."
ANTHONY HOPKINS

THE YOUNG, DARKLY HANDSOME Brit first made his name in Hollywood as a heartthrob, playing a succession of dashing, cryptic archetypes—Heathcliff in 'Wuthering Heights,' Darcy in 'Pride and Prejudice,' Maxim de Winter in 'Rebecca.' But it wasn't until Laurence Olivier returned to England that he truly made his mark, by bringing to the screen (as both star and director) the classical virtuosity he had already exhibited on stage. His triumphant, Technicolor 'Henry V' (1944) and his noirish 'Hamlet' (1948) set a benchmark for film acting. Even in later years, as his movie work dwindled, the regal grace Olivier brought to Hollywood projects like 1976's 'Marathon Man' allowed popcorn munchers a glimpse of that special something usually enjoyed only by theatergoers: sheer theatrical brilliance. —Nisid Hajari

Laurence Olivier

Dustin Hoffman

HOFFMAN ONCE JESTED that he became an actor in order to get laid. That may seem an odd catalyst for one of the screen's virtuoso performers—a man whose diligent perfectionism, highly developed range, and history of struggle all affirm the almost holy esteem in which he holds his calling. But for a star who specializes in the unglamorous, that half joke is totally in character.

Hoffman's first major film role, in 1967, immediately established his antihero credentials: As Benjamin Braddock in 'The Graduate,' he wore his passivity like a generational badge, earning himself an Oscar nomination and a slew of offers to play disenchanted youths. He was already 30 at the time, having immigrated to New York from his native Los Angeles to become the classic starving artist. So when he chose the vulpine Ratso Rizzo in John Schlesinger's 'Midnight Cowboy' as his follow-up role in 1969 (earning a second Oscar nomination), he set off on what was, for him, a more appropriate course—one that ran against the grain.

In the following decades, his hangdog leads and obsessively insecure heroes would assume forms as diverse as the cross-dressing Michael Dorsey in 'Tootsie' (1982) and the autistic Raymond in 'Rain Man' (1988). And Hoffman's devotion to craft—an urge to control that irked many a director—would become legendary. For all the accolades he has received as a master thespian, his greatness actually lies in his ability to put staunchly little lives up on the big screen. (Photograph by Steve Schapiro)—NH

THOUGH SHE STUDIED MIME in Paris, Lange has always traded upon a unique—and uniquely damaged—heartland appeal. After a disastrous debut in 1976's 'King Kong,' she worked her open, gracious beauty to advantage in two divergent films: as Dustin Hoffman's wary foil in 1982's 'Tootsie,' and as the doomed actress Frances Farmer in 'Frances' the same year. (She was nominated for Oscars in both, winning Best Supporting Actress for 'Tootsie.') Lange's variations on strong women have gained repeated Academy notice, but as her Oscar-winning turn as the tormented matriarch of 'Blue Sky' (1994) indicates, it's the fragility under that strength—the emotions fluttering like trapped birds under her prairie-sky gaze—that haunt you long after the lights come up. (Photograph by Firooz Zahedi)—NH

"He's always saying, 'Let's try that scene again.' When a scene starts to fly, unpredictable things start to happen."
NICOLE KIDMAN, on Hoffman

Jessica Lange

ESSENTIAL LANGE

FRANCES
(1982) As tragic Hollywood victim Frances Farmer, Lange erased all memories of 'King Kong'—and got one of her two 1982 Oscar nominations.

TOOTSIE
(1982) And here's the role for which she won, as the damaged but delightful love interest of in-drag Dustin Hoffman.

COUNTRY
(1984) One of three farm dramas that year, but the one that made the most lasting impression. She coproduced and, with real-life love Sam Shepard, costarred.

MEN DON'T LEAVE
(1990) Little-seen but one of her best, with Lange radiantly coming apart at the seams as a widowed mom who tries to put it all back together.

BLUE SKY
(1994) Another Oscar win as Tommy Lee Jones' Army wife, toeing the line between the unconventional and the insane.

ESSENTIAL HOFFMAN

THE GRADUATE
(1967) He smartly played Benjamin Braddock as a cipher—and an entire generation filled in the blanks.

MIDNIGHT COWBOY
(1969) Determined to avoid youth parts, Hoffman found the soul in a consumptive Times Square hustler and proved himself as an artist.

LITTLE BIG MAN
(1970) Arthur Penn's epic anti-Western is full of brilliant noise, yet Hoffman is its canny center as ultimate survivor Jack Crabb.

TOOTSIE
(1982) On screen and off, it's about an actor taking a ridiculously farfetched dare and making it work perfectly.

RAIN MAN
(1988) An Oscar-winning performance of technical genius, but the star is careful to show us the man behind the scrim of autism.

Meryl Streep

"There's simply no finer craftsman in the business. She's as good as it gets." ROBERT REDFORD

ESSENTIAL STREEP

THE FRENCH LIEUTENANT'S WOMAN

(1981) Bewitching as both a scandalous 19th-century lady and the woman playing her in a film, Streep got her first Best Actress nomination.

SOPHIE'S CHOICE

(1982) She won the next year as a tragically damaged Holocaust survivor beloved by both Kevin Kline and Peter MacNicol.

SILKWOOD

(1983, above) Nominated again for a daringly raunchy depiction of blue-collar whistle-blower—and no-nukes martyr—Karen Silkwood.

OUT OF AFRICA

(1985) And again for finding the complicated heart of author Isak Dinesen, a.k.a. Karen Blixen, growing coffee and wooing Redford in colonial Kenya.

THE BRIDGES OF MADISON COUNTY

(1995) And yet again—her 10th Oscar nomination to

SHE DOES NOT—cannot—pander, and so Meryl Streep is viewed with a certain mistrust by a large segment of the moviegoing public. She's the movie star as medicine: good for you, but not much fun. There's her angular WASP remove, and a name that sounds like the sigh of a conflicted goose. She inhabits her roles with a craft that can occasionally seem academic. Worst of all—oh, much worse—she refuses to play the movie star off screen, and what kind of star is that?

The kind for whom acting is simply, incandescently, its own reward. She has received 10 Oscar nominations and won twice (for 1979's 'Kramer vs. Kramer' and 1982's 'Sophie's Choice'), racking up the highest total of any actress since Katharine Hepburn and Bette Davis. Statuettes, though, only hint at the rich human truths Streep delivers in films like 'The French Lieutenant's Woman' (1981) or 'Out of Africa' (1985). With the comedy of 'She-Devil' (1989) and 'Death Becomes Her' (1992) and the action of 'The River Wild' (1994), she is clearly trying to limber up, maybe even win over those who hate medicine. Good for her, but she really needn't bother. Streep remains a brilliant artisan whose specialty is headstrong, sometimes wrongheaded women. Deal with it. (Photograph by Brian Aris) —TB

Robert DeNiro

"ARE YOU TALKIN' to me?" Travis Bickle's seething monologue in Martin Scorsese's 'Taxi Driver' (1976) challenges not only his mirror, but his audience: The terror inspired by De Niro's performance, possibly the most towering of 1970s American cinema, awakens visceral doubts—perhaps we are complicit with his rage, and the barrier between screen and viewer might not be so firm.

Although the influence of Method mavens Stella Adler and Lee Strasberg on De Niro's work is clear—witness the pounds he packed on for his Oscar-winning performance as boxer Jake La Motta in 1980's 'Raging Bull'—his skill goes beyond realism. He also won an Oscar for his searing portrayal of the young Vito Corleone in Francis Ford Coppola's 'The Godfather, Part II' (1974) and was nominated for his role in Michael Cimino's Vietnam drama 'The Deer Hunter' (1978). But he is perhaps most successful at crystallizing our dark impulses through the characters created with Scorsese: a small-time hood in 1973's 'Mean Streets,' the obsessive fan in 1983's 'The King of Comedy,' the vengeful ex-con in 1991's 'Cape Fear,' the volatile mobster accountant in 1995's 'Casino'—highly charged individuals who take their feelings too far. Like no other actor today, he knows how to draw a mythic character uncomfortably close to the moviegoer's own capacity for losing control. (Photograph by Anne Marie Fox) —NH

Richard Burton

ONCE CONSIDERED the heir to Olivier, Burton suffered both greater scrutiny and lesser acclaim because of the love of a woman. The Oxford-educated Welshman with the resonant baritone prepared himself for Hollywood on the English stage. And his early films—such as 'My Cousin Rachel' (1952) and 'The Robe' (1953), both of which earned him Oscar nominations—bear witness to his natural charisma. After he took up with Elizabeth Taylor on the set of 1963's 'Cleopatra,' Olivier asked him whether he wanted to be an actor or a household name. Burton's reply: "Both." And, indeed, when films like 'Who's Afraid of Virginia Woolf?' (1966) shed the glamour of their pairing, it's clear he succeeded in plying a craft that outshone even La Liz's diamonds. —NH

"He was marvelous at rehearsals. There was the true theatrical instinct. You only had to indicate. Scarcely even that." JOHN GIELGUD on Burton

CARL LAEMMLE presents

Lombard

Like all the great movie comedians, Carole Lombard was a genius at making a fool of herself—how many glam queens would be willing to sport such a shiner?—and suffered pratfalls galore as a society girl in 1936's 'Love Before Breakfast'

COMEDY IS NOT pretty. In other chapters of this book, you'll find leading men of manly jaw and rippling pecs; distinguishing features here, by contrast, are Groucho's mustache, Stan Laurel's idiot grin, Woody Allen's what-me-worry shrug. Is it that we extend celebrity to the unhandsome only when they make us laugh? In other words, is Hollywood the ultimate high school cafeteria? Or is it that the great physical comedians are the average man's attachés in Valhalla, walking among the gods and goddesses of the cinema and sticking matches between their toes?

Not all comics are pure silliness, of course. Jack Lemmon, Robin Williams, and Eddie Murphy have each played it straight, their reined-in high spirits often adding to the dramatic tension. What's interesting, though, is that their first impulses are almost always comic. Lemmon's fussy neuroses, Williams' helpless channel surfing, Murphy's aggressive funk are all as valid as valor in a conventional leading man—just more inventive and unexpected. We laugh because heroes aren't supposed to be this clever, aren't supposed to cast doubt on the whole notion of heroism.

So there are the goons and comedic actors—where are the women? Largely shut out by the Hollywood factory, sad to say. Yes, Lucille Ball may be the greatest comedian, male or female, in TV history, but she had to go to TV to realize her gift; after 20 years in the movies, her persona still hadn't jelled. Carole Lombard is here because, alone among the great Hollywood beauties, she had a supreme gift for raucous, playing-with-the-boys comedy. And despite more funny ladies than ever in today's movies, it's still a man's mad, mad world. Okay, comedy is not pretty—but who says pretty can't be comedy? —Ty Burr

CHAPLIN MAY RANK higher here (it's hard to downgrade the very first global superstar), but Keaton quite possibly carries a greater relevance to audiences today. It's not just that Chaplin's sentimentality looks a little creaky now next to Buster's wary calm. It's that in our increasingly mechanized world, Keaton's work makes sense. His comedies pit a lone, baffled hero against huge, impersonal forces—a tornado in 'Steamboat Bill, Jr.' (1928), an empty ocean liner in 'The Navigator' (1924), the movement of trains and armies in 'The General' (1927). His films are about movement, in fact: The laughs invariably come as his sudden grace flashes against a background of unreasoning, geometric process.

His career, sadly, was a similar flash of grace. A child star in vaudeville, Keaton rose through the slapstick-film world as a second banana to Fatty Arbuckle, eventually making a production deal with Metro that gave him free rein. He made 37 shorts and 11 features—many brilliant, all hilarious—before drinking, divorce, and the loss of creative control sent him tumbling into the has-been bin just as talkies came chattering onto the screen. With his films at last on tape after decades of delay, home video saves Keaton's legacy: a grave beauty, a stuntman's poise, and a resigned comic wisdom that seems more modern with each year. —TB

"The lyric poet
of the silent screen"
MARION MEADE,
Keaton biographer

Buster
Keaton

ABBOTT AND COSTELLO, Martin and Lewis, Kramden and Norton, Oscar and Felix. Most of the great comedy teams sprang from the almost accidental pairing in 1926 of Stan Laurel, a British-born former understudy to Charlie Chaplin, and Oliver Hardy, a onetime child minstrel in his native Georgia. Director Leo McCarey saw possibilities in teaming the thin, childlike Laurel with the rotund, pompous Hardy, and the two would go on to make more than 100 movies together. Audiences loved their familiar slapstick antics, but fans also thrilled to their dark humor and silent asides. Buster Keaton's films had more wit, perhaps, and Chaplin's more art. Laurel and Hardy simply got more laughs. —Steve Wulf

La

"In 104 films, they never ran out of comic ideas, insane invention, charming conceits"
GARSON KANIN, screenwriter

Hardy

ESSENTIAL ALLEN

BANANAS

(1971) A nebbish turns dictator for love. A messy, low-budget, anarchic pratfall of a movie—and side-splittingly funny.

SLEEPER

(1973) The best and most confident of his early comedies. Woody wakes up in the future, romances Diane Keaton, and jousts with giant vegetables.

ANNIE HALL

(1977) In which the comic genius matured into a wise, aware chronicler of modern romance. To some, it's all been downhill since.

ZELIG

(1983) It's the most fantastic of conceits—a man so shy he physically mutates to resemble those around him— so how come the movie resonates with profundity?

HANNAH AND HER SISTERS

(1986) He was starting to look out of place in his own films, but the scene where he rediscovers life by watching 'Duck Soup' is a joy.

ESSENTIAL MARX BROTHERS

MONKEY BUSINESS

(1931) Finally breaking free of the staginess of their first two films, the boys take to the open seas in herring barrels.

HORSE FEATHERS

(1932) Groucho goes to college, academia goes to the dogs, and each brother gets a crack at singing "Everyone Says I Love You."

DUCK SOUP

(1933) Groucho takes over as president of Freedonia and plunges the country into war. Too dark for its day, it looks right on the money now.

A NIGHT AT THE OPERA

(1935) The brothers' first for MGM, and the anarchy of the Paramount films gets tamed. But how can you argue with the stateroom scene?

A NIGHT IN CASABLANCA

(1946) After a string of duds, the Marxes came through late in the day with a paralyzingly funny spoof on that movie with Humphrey what's-his-name.

BY THE EARLY '80s, Allen had already become the chief chronicler of Uppereastsideus Americanus, occasionally on target, just as often maddeningly precious. But in the '70s, he looked to be the one true heir to Groucho, with 'Bananas' (1971) and 'Sleeper' (1973). And 1977's Oscar favorite, 'Annie Hall,' is still one profoundly hilarious relationship movie. Allen has moved away from appearing in his films, to the point where he actually served as a distraction in the otherwise stunning 'Crimes and Misdemeanors' (1989). But he is a key star of his time: insistently cerebral, irresolvably horny, and courting deeper meaning with a spit-take. (Photograph by Philippe Halsman) —TB

Woody
Allen

"They say Woody Allen got something from the Marx Brothers. He didn't. He is an original. The best. The funniest."
GROUCHO MARX

RISING UP FROM the vaudeville circuit like a hydra-headed 'tummler,' the three key Marxes united different schools of comedy in one brutal assault. Harpo looked back to the silent slapstick of Chaplin and Keaton, Groucho wielded the aggressive verbosity of the 'New Yorker'/Broadway/Algonquin axis, and Chico leveled the field with dimly insistent vaudeville shtick. They made five demented comedies for Paramount before MGM tamed them with romantic leads and sappy songs; the high-water mark is probably 'Duck Soup' (1933), a political farce so acutely silly that it had to wait for the 1960s to be appreciated. —TB

Jack Lemmon

HIS MADCAP DRAG ACT in 1959's 'Some Like It Hot' shot him to the top of the comic A list, and he's been there ever since (often in the sidesplitting company of his buddy Walter Matthau). But what truly sets Lemmon apart is the dark side of that quicksilver talent: When he reaches deep down into his soul—as he did to play the raging drunk in 'Days of Wine and Roses' (1962) or the anguished whistle-blower in 'The China Syndrome' (1979) or the desperate father seeking his son in 'Missing' (1982)—the results are heartbreaking. Whether serious or silly, his specialty has always been the neurotic bundle of nerves at odds with the modern world—trembling with rage but always engaging. No other Lemmon ever tasted so sweet. (Photography by Julian Wasser)—Michael Sauter

"His genius was so riveting that I would often come in on my days off just to watch him cast his comic spell before the camera" SHIRLEY MACLAINE on Lemmon

NO AMERICAN MOVIE star owes so much to the exigencies of war. A master of the topical joke, Hope has always fared best when playing against major events. Unsurprisingly, then, it was an audience sobered by World War II that first seized upon Hope's singular brand of comic cowardice, his renditions of con artists always ready to turn tail. That wiseacre shtick lodged Hope securely among Hollywood's top 10 moneymakers from 1941 to 1953. In the smash-hit 'Road' pictures, America found a soothing silliness in his buffoonish partnership with Bing Crosby, though his pairing with Jane Russell in the Western spoof 'The Paleface' (1948) made him the country's No. 1 star—and sealed his future as a bona fide American institution. (Photography by Philippe Halsman)—Nisid Hajari

Bob Hope

ESSENTIAL HOPE

THE GHOST BREAKERS

(1940) Hope was always funniest playing yellow, and this haunted-house comedy with Paulette Goddard will make you blue with laughter.

ROAD TO MOROCCO

(1942) The best of the Hope-Crosby 'Road' movies? Hard to pick one, but this outrageous sand saga may be the most emblematic.

MONSIEUR BEAUCAIRE

(1946) Bob cuts hair and dons wigs as an 18th-century French barber masquerading as a courtly fop.

THE PALEFACE

(1948) Hope meets pistol-packin' Jane Russell in this hilarious Western parody. PC it ain't; funny it is.

BEAU JAMES

(1957) A rare straight—if still high-flying—role as bon vivant James Walker, New York's mayor during the Roaring '20s.

ESSENTIAL LEMMON

SOME LIKE IT HOT

(1959) Sure, this classic is gut-funny, but Lemmon finds a flighty freedom in drag that's positively subversive for the '50s.

THE APARTMENT

(1960) Billy Wilder's farce lets the star play the ultimate company man: a schnook who lends his pad out for "executive action."

DAYS OF WINE AND ROSES

(1962) A chipper ad exec who drags himself and wife Lee Remick into alcoholism. It still looks to be his darkest, least mannered performance.

THE ODD COUPLE

(1968) All the nervous-Nellie Lemmon tics are wrapped up with a bow in his role as Felix Unger, opposite eternal foil Walter Matthau as Oscar.

GLENGARRY GLEN ROSS

(1992) A '90s triumph as a desperate real estate salesman in the caustic film version of David Mamet's play.

ESSENTIAL LOMBARD

TWENTIETH CENTURY
(1934) A perfectly insane
Howard Hawks farce,
with Lombard and John
Barrymore like whirling
dervishes as a stage producer
and his battling star.

MY MAN GODFREY
(1936) Her poor little rich
girl who hires suave bum
William Powell as a butler is
one of the screen's enduring
flibbertigibbets.

NOTHING SACRED
(1937) Pretending to be dying
of radium poisoning, she
suckers New York into falling
at her feet—and trades
punches with Fredric March.

SWING HIGH, SWING LOW
(1937) A rare non-comedic
Lombard, in a sexy—and
ultimately heartbreaking—
romance from underrated
director Mitchell Leisen.

TO BE OR NOT TO BE
(1942) A hilariously vain
actress helping hammy
husband Jack Benny
outthink the Nazis—and,
sadly, her final role.

ESSENTIAL MURPHY

48 HRS.
(1982) He came out of 'SNL'
to conquer the world. The
whole movie's a hoot, but his
redneck-bar standoff
served notice that a new
star had arrived.

BEVERLY HILLS COP
(1984) The moment of grace:
Eddie still looked like an
underdog, and this slam-bang
fish-out-of-water action farce
was a massive hit.

EDDIE MURPHY RAW
(1987) Returning to the
stand-up stage for a sizzling
concert film that captures
him at his comedic best—and
foulmouthed worst.

COMING TO AMERICA
(1988) After a string of
smug misfires, he came off
his action throne for a sweet
farce about a king (African)
lost in Queens (New York).

THE NUTTY PROFESSOR
(1996) The long-awaited
comedy comeback, with
the star showing a new
gentleness as a portly prof
whose potion turns him
into—well, Eddie Murphy.

Carole
Lombard

SUCH WAS THE GIDDY glamour of Lombard that she could do a pratfall in an evening gown or look stunning with an ice pack on her head. Whether playing a temperamental Broadway diva in 'Twentieth Century' (1934), a giddy heiress in 'My Man Godfrey' (1936), or an ambivalent con artist in 'Nothing Sacred' (1937), she relished making a splendid fool of herself. Behind the screen, she was a classic guy's gal (Fred MacMurray said of her: "Swore like a man—other women try, but she really did"), and it was not too surprising when she married the classic man's man, Clark Gable, in 1939. Three years later, she died at 33 in a wartime plane crash, an early exit that stands as one of the damnedest shames in movie history. —MS

MURPHY WAS THE RAUNCHIEST trickster of the '80s, throwing the decade's casual racism back in its face and reaping millions for his pains. Years in stand-up and on 'Saturday Night Live'—his characters remain the most subversive in the show's history—cultivated his unique appeal: a humor both obsequious and in-your-face. After '48 HRS.' (1982) and 'Beverly Hills Cop' (1984), he seemed to rule the world. But nothing's less funny than a comic who treats his audience like subjects, and later films saw diminishing returns. Still, this is not a talent to just go away, and 1992's 'Boomerang' saw a maturity that blossomed with gentle hilarity in 1996's 'The Nutty Professor.' It's a comeback more satisfying for having come out of nowhere. (Photograph by Alastair Thain)—TB

Eddie
Murphy

"His effect is dazzling. There's a ding when he walks on, almost like Marilyn Monroe." JOHN LANDIS, director

"Robin embodies
everything about the
child inside of us"
STEVEN SPIELBERG

Bing
Crosb

CROSBY SEEMED FATED for a screen life of on-the-road high jinks with Bob Hope, but one day his golfing buddy, director Leo McCarey, decided to ordain him. "Now what kind of a priest could I play?" the popular crooner countered. "I'd be unbelievable." Crosby, of course, became baseball-loving Father O'Malley in 'Going My Way' (1944), the sentimental favorite that won him an Oscar. He was such a believable priest, in fact, that he was also nominated for the sequel, The 'Bells of St. Mary's.' Every once in a while, der Bingle stepped outside his persona, as he did with admirable restraint and vulnerability playing the drunken has-been in 'The Country Girl' (1954). But when he put on that collar of affability, people flocked to see him. (Photograph by Talmage Morrison) —SW

Robin
Williams

THERE IS NO PRECEDENT for Robin Williams in Hollywood history—maybe not in human history. There's some of Danny Kaye's lightness, Jerry Lewis' spastic intensity, Chaplin's gravity, Groucho's verbal swordsmanship, Jonathan Winters' moonbeam anarchy, but none of them seemed so possessed by the demons of comic dissonance. When Williams is "on"—in 'Good Morning, Vietnam' (1987), in 'The Fisher King' (1991), and above all in his free-fall stand-up specials—it is as if his synapses are colliding with joy. His most representative role may have been the one in which he was totally freed from his body: As the voice of the Genie in Disney's animated 'Aladdin' (1992), he was given free rein to mutate into whomever he chose (all the animators had to do was connect the dots).

However, to his credit and to his fans' occasional dismay, he has always had more in mind than comedy. Williams' second film after the success of TV's 'Mork & Mindy' was 1982's 'The World According to Garp,' and the weary kindliness of that role is a hat he has chosen to wear often: in 'Moscow on the Hudson' (1984), 'Dead Poets Society' (1989), 'Awakenings' (1990). 'Mrs. Doubtfire' (1993) saw the two sides come together for broad comedy and uneasy sentiment, but 'The Birdcage' (1996) was further proof of Williams' range and depth. His subject, it is becoming clear, is human dignity—and the brilliant fireworks that can shoot up in its absence. (Photograph by Alastair Thain) —TB

Shirley Temple was at
the height of her fame
when she made 1937's
'Wee Willie Winkie.'
Bright-eyed, curly-
topped, and dimpled,
she may be the ultimate
ingenue, winning the
day against all odds
with a combination of
naïveté and pluck.

The ngenues

THE INGENUE'S LOT—the burden of carrying innocence forward in a world inclined to either enshrine or mock it—is an unenviable one. And it may be hardest of all for the true ingenues, the child stars. Growing up is difficult enough without doing it in front of millions of people watching from the dark. For Judy Garland, it turned out to be impossible: In her singing, even late in life, you can hear the endless search for a lost simplicity. Shirley Temple was luckier: Always the most natural, least self-conscious of kiddie stars, she turned into a pleasant, bland adult presence with no future in movies and no wish to have one. And Natalie Wood may have been luckiest: By the time she entered a turbulent adolescence, audiences were ready to see realistically troubled teens on the screen. Who knows? Maybe Garland would have been saved if she had been the right age for 'Rebel Without a Cause' instead of the wrong age for 'The Wizard of Oz.'

There are also grown women who have gripped the torch of sweetness and light. In the silent era, Lillian Gish and Mary Pickford were the chief embodiments of goodness, Gish through the clear-eyed honesty of her acting, Pickford through the hardheaded decision to play little girls into her 30s. By the late 1950s and early '60s, the ingenue was tightly clasped by the old guard and ridiculed by the new youth. The final representatives of the type, Doris Day and Julie Andrews, had stellar careers playing sweetie pies, but it's worth noting that both women are more complex actresses than their critics—and even they themselves—have often acknowledged. You think it's easy being the last virgins in Hollywood?—Ty Burr

HER VOICE COULD have received its own billing: Powerful yet tremulous, it possessed a dramatic personality the equal of any great actor. In 1939, when she was 17, those pipes became internationally known when 'The Wizard of Oz' transported the former Frances Gumm as far into the stratosphere as her ruby-slippered character. Garland's star continued to soar from her teens into adulthood, bookended by the hits 'Meet Me in St. Louis' (1944) and 'A Star Is Born' (1954). Her personal difficulties throughout are well documented, but they seem only to have magnified her ability to immerse herself in sentimental material. That we know the quiver in her voice is real makes its touch all the more sharp. (Photograph by Dennis Stock) —Nisid Hajari

Judy

Garland

"The finest all-round performer we ever had in America was Judy Garland. There was no limit to her talent." GENE KELLY

ESSENTIAL GARLAND

THE WIZARD OF OZ
(1939, below) Vulnerable, courageous, full of yearning, her Dorothy has a mythic resonance for millions of Baby Boomers.

MEET ME IN ST. LOUIS
(1944) Still one of the most enchanting of movie musicals, with Garland singing a heart-stopping "Have Yourself a Merry Little Christmas."

THE CLOCK
(1945) Under the direction of soon-to-be-husband Vincente Minnelli, she stars in an elegantly simple Manhattan romance.

EASTER PARADE
(1948) Mix Garland and Fred Astaire, add Irving Berlin tunes like "A Couple of Swells," stir, sit back, and enjoy.

A STAR IS BORN
(1954) It's James Mason's character who falls apart, but Garland's offscreen struggles give the film an unbearably moving subtext.

Lillian Gish

AS LONG AS Gish was alive, so was the entire, century-long history of the movies; with her passing at age 97 in 1993, there was finally no one left to say "This is how it was." Working for mentor D.W. Griffith in such groundbreaking films as 'The Birth of a Nation' (1915) and 'Way Down East' (1920), Gish combined the beauty of a Victorian cameo with an unflinching emotional honesty. In the process, she virtually invented modern screen acting. She retreated to the stage when sound came in, but returned, memorably, as a deceptively frail force of good in the scarifying 'The Night of the Hunter' (1955). Her greatest role was in 'The Wind' (1928), as a prairie heroine battling the elements, and in truth, you felt that Gish's firm, gracious kindness could have kept a tornado at bay. —TB

"She was the young
girl every man wanted
to have—as his sister"
ALISTAIR COOKE,
on Pickford

BARELY REMEMBERED now with the passing of time and fashion, Pickford was once, simply, the most powerful person in Hollywood. One of the first movie stars, she caught the public's fancy as early as 1910. Her plucky Little Mary persona—in films like 'Pollyanna' (1920) and 'Little Lord Fauntleroy' (1921)—was even more globally popular than Chaplin's Tramp. Pickford was also a brilliant businesswoman who managed her own career (Sam Goldwyn noted acidly that it took longer to make her contracts than her pictures), directed many of her own films, cofounded and ran United Artists, and retired at the age of 40 a millionaire many times over. "The little girl made me," she said later. "I wasn't waiting for the little girl to kill me." (Photograph by Nelson Evans) —TB

Mary Pickford

ESSENTIAL WOOD

MIRACLE ON 34TH STREET
(1947) At 9, Wood was the very soul of jaded New York childhood, hoping against hope to believe in Kriss Kringle.

REBEL WITHOUT A CAUSE
(1955) Matching James Dean stride for swooning cynical stride in Nick Ray's ever-timely teenage-wasteland classic.

SPLENDOR IN THE GRASS
(1961) Her most melodramatic role—and maybe her greatest—as a star-crossed lover who goes mad for Warren Beatty.

WEST SIDE STORY
(1961) Okay, so Wood is about as Puerto Rican as Doris Day. Still, singing "There's a Place for Us," she's a heartrendingly believable Maria.

LOVE WITH THE PROPER STRANGER
(1963) It's as if the little girl from 'Miracle' matured into a smart, tough New Yorker who has to rediscover romance when Steve McQueen gets her pregnant.

ESSENTIAL DAY

LOVE ME OR LEAVE ME
(1955) If you thought she always played Miss Innocent, check out this tawdry true-life saloon tale with Jimmy Cagney.

THE MAN WHO KNEW TOO MUCH
(1956) She sings "Que Sera Sera"—a lot—and rescues her child from kidnappers in this lush Hitchcock thriller.

THE PAJAMA GAME
(1957) In a delightful musical romp, she's a factory grievance committee head falling—with much "Steam Heat"—for foreman John Raitt.

PILLOW TALK
(1959) Doris and Rock Hudson chatting via phone and via split screen while in their bathtubs was as sexy as it got in 1959.

LOVER COME BACK
(1961) The Day-Hudson teaming really sparks in this hilarious comedy about ad execs stealing each others' clients and hearts.

Day

"When I first saw her, I detected behind the well-mannered, young wife front a desperate twinkle in her eyes. I knew there was an unsatisfied hunger there."
ELIA KAZAN, on Wood

AN ELFIN BEAUTY who began her career at age 5, Wood advanced through every phase possible, from kid star (in 1947's 'Miracle on 34th Street') to martyred adult. Jumping into 'Rebel Without a Cause' at 17 might have seemed a risky transition to screen adulthood, but it worked: Not only did Wood earn a 1955 Oscar nomination, but the film's brazen message of teen disillusionment ensured she would never be pigeonholed as a moppet. Fortunately, her cuteness lingered. And if the sexual intensity of films such as 'Splendor in the Grass' (1961) emphasized the heat simmering behind those dark features (only Hollywood could have taken her for Puerto Rican, yet she made Maria her own in 1961's 'West Side Story'), the playfulness with which she treated sex in later social comedies (like 1969's 'Bob & Carol & Ted & Alice') succeeded because it hinted at the kid who still lived there as well. (Photograph by Lee Balterman) —NH

Natalie
Wood

WHEN SHE WAS just a little girl, Doris von Kappelhoff asked her stage mother, "What will I be?" Mama said, "A dancer," but after a car accident badly injured her right leg, Doris became a singer and took her stage name from the song "Day by Day." Legendary Hollywood wit Oscar Levant once said, "I knew Doris Day before she was a virgin." Day did have a sunny sex appeal as a sort of anti-Monroe, and she eventually starred as the bedroom quarry of Rock Hudson in a series of middle-brow sex farces ('Pillow Talk,' 'Lover Come Back,' 'Send Me No Flowers'). She received an Oscar nomination in 1959 for 'Pillow Talk,' but was actually much better in 'Love Me or Leave Me' (1955)—her song "Mean to Me" describes her own disastrous personal life—and Hitchcock's 'The Man Who Knew Too Much' (1956). In the latter, she sang her anthem, "Que Sera Sera." Her fate, it's clear, was to be a star. —Steve Wulf

Shirley Temple

HOW BIG was little Shirley Temple? Her father received propositions from women hoping against genetic hope to beget another Shirley. When she lost her front tooth in an on-set accident, studio chief Darryl Zanuck panicked and raced out of a meeting with John Steinbeck. When she sat in the lap of a department-store Santa, he asked for her autograph. Temple was the No. 1 box office star from 1935 to 1938—from age 7 to 10—and her buoyant can-do attitude was a psychic lifeline to a nation mired in the Depression. Her grown-up peers could only look on in slightly creeped-out awe. Said Alice Faye: "She knew everyone's dialogue, and if you forgot a line, she gave it to you. We all hated her for that." Her films have grown dated, but her assured adorableness lives on. —TB

THESE ARE A FEW of our favorite things about Julie Andrews: singing and spinning merrily atop a mountain in Bavaria (and, not coincidentally, turning 1965's 'The Sound of Music' into the most popular movie musical of all time) and using her plucky British charm and impeccable manners to transcend the inherent corniness of a supercalifragilisticexpialidocious role like Mary Poppins (and earning an Oscar in the process). Ultimately, she turned her squeaky-clean image on its ear by baring her breasts in 1981's 'S.O.B.' and playing a woman who is pretending to be a man who's pretending to be a woman in 1982's 'Victor/Victoria.' She returned to that role and her stage roots in the current Broadway adaptation. Throughout it all, she's been music to our ears. (Photograph by Gene Lester)—David Hochman

Julie Andrews

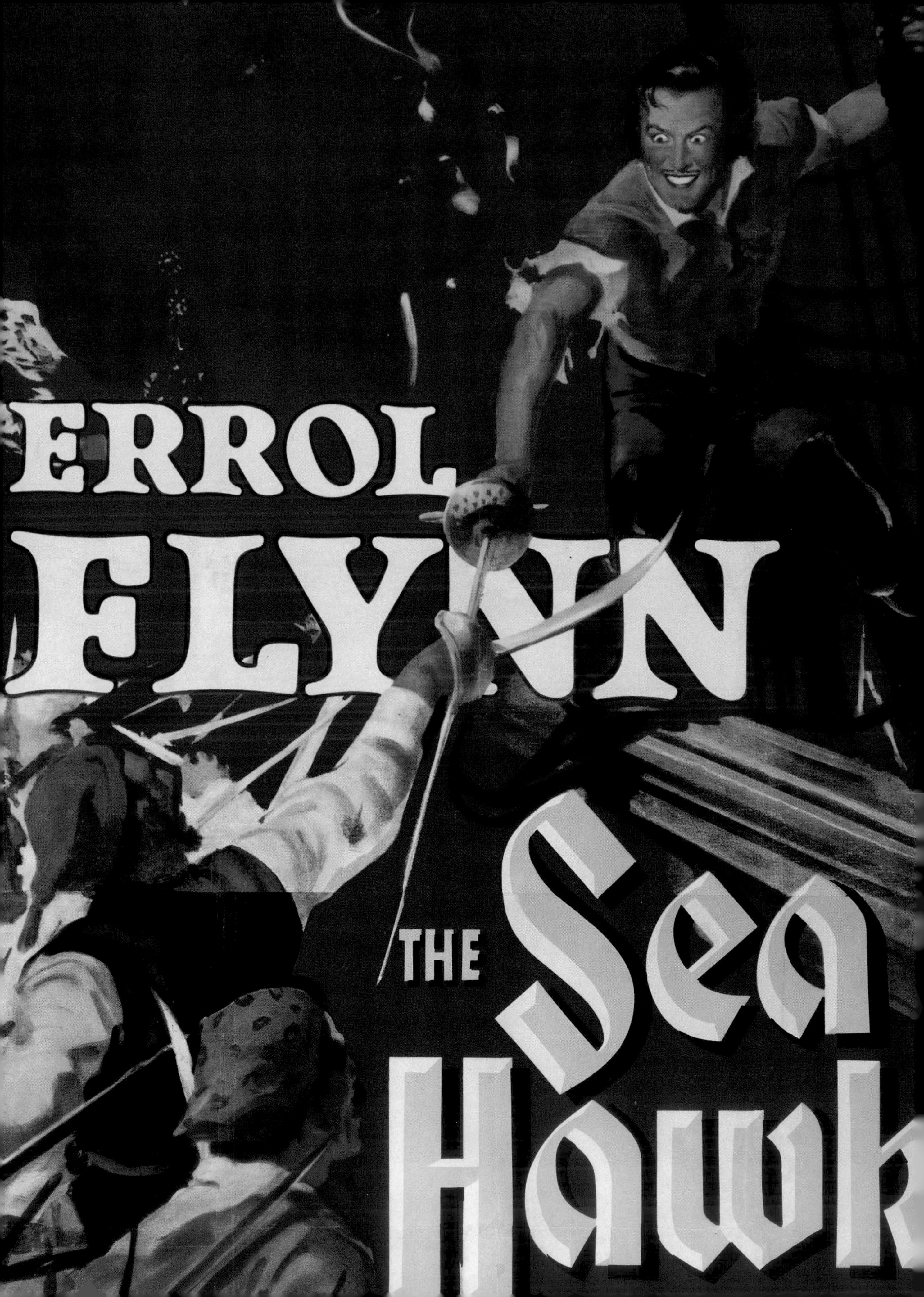
ERROL
FLYNN
THE
Sea
Hawk

The Action Heroes

THE LEADING MAN solves conflicts with panache; the tough guy by throwing a punch; the everyguy with drawling sincerity. Action heroes just blow everything to hell.

Well, they do nowadays, even if they haven't always been no-neck colossi like Arnold. Along with the movies, the type has evolved—if that's the correct verb—in the direction of bigger, brawnier, louder. The fine rapier wit of Errol Flynn has given way to the blunt Uzi ironies of Sly Stallone, and if we get our moviegoing money's worth in detonations and blood squibs, it's hard to dispute that some niceties have been lost in the crossfire.

The first action hero was Douglas Fairbanks Sr., who evinced a dandy's merriment that would probably have today's hunks beating him up after class. But Fairbanks seemed as much a special effect to audiences in the '20s as Schwarzenegger does to his: leaping, grinning, flying through the air on magic carpets, he appeared to defy gravity. Flynn extended that devil-may-care deadliness into the sound era, but the post-WWII era saw a newer, glummer breed of beef: Charlton Heston and Kirk Douglas got the job done, but it looked like it killed them to do it.

As James Bond, Sean Connery brought style back into the equation, but his lasting legacy may have been to point the action hero in the direction of the comic strip. Thus Mel, Arnold, and Sly are Connery's heirs; they offer no subtlety, nor do we ask it of them. Of late, though, the wheel has started to turn once more: Keanu Reeves and Nicolas Cage have both buffed up while keeping their spacy dude-osity intact, and Bruce Willis has melded the action hero with the everyguy in a fashion that gets more interesting with every picture. A he-man with nuance? Now, that's a killer. —Ty Burr

An early action hero in action, Flynn exemplified the traits that are still essential to daredevil stars: an athletic figure, a raffish attitude—and nerves of steel

CONNERY HAD THE RARE LUCK (and, all right, the skill) to both define a role and transcend it. He is the quintessential James Bond for most people, and not merely because he was there first. In the Ian Fleming novels, Agent 007 is a jokey, supremely efficient upper-class Brit—what a backroom Cold War bureaucrat could only dream of being—but the young Scot added a blue-collar arrogance to the role that, in retrospect, was necessary. Connery's Bond has an innate cruelty that comes from a knowledge of his own superiority, yet he is light-footed enough to roll with the campy punches (and dagger-tipped kicks, and razor-edged hats). No other Bond has ever managed to be in on the joke and also rise above it.

Terence Young, who directed three early Bond films, has spoken of Connery's disdain for stardom and his concern with "personal integrity," but audiences were on to that from the start. It's why the public has allowed him to have a post-007 career, why smaller films like 'A Fine Madness' (1966) have been accepted and outright flops like—sorry, Sean—'Cuba' (1979) and 'Wrong Is Right' (1982) are forgiven. His finest later roles—in 'The Man Who Would Be King' (1975), 'Robin and Marian' (1976), 'The Untouchables' (1987), and the last Indiana Jones film in 1989—add human details to a portrait begun with Bond. His heroes, no longer invincible, remain unbowed. —TB

Sean
Connery

"When you're with Sean, you learn pretty quickly what your own place in the galaxy is—and it pales" KEVIN COSTNER

Steve McQueen

"Once I asked him, 'Why do you ride those motorcycles like that and maybe kill yourself?' and he said, 'So I won't forget I'm a man and not just an actor.'" BETTE DAVIS

ESSENTIAL MCQUEEN

THE GREAT ESCAPE
(1963) He aims his motorcycle at freedom—and upstages a huge international cast—in this classic WWII actioner.

LOVE WITH THE PROPER STRANGER
(1963) Surpassingly tender as a saxophonist trying to do the right thing by pregnant one-night stand Natalie Wood.

BABY THE RAIN MUST FALL
(1965) It fell between the cracks at the time, but McQueen's performance as an ex-con trying to make good now looks like a winner.

BULLITT
(1968, above) Filmmakers are still ripping off the car chases, and actors are still imitating McQueen as the cynical city detective.

THE THOMAS CROWN AFFAIR
(1968) An engaging heist film that now looks to be a wonderfully silly exhibit for the '60s time capsule.

HE WAS UNIQUE among the bankable stars of his day: a rugged action hero with serious actor credentials. Though he made his name in Westerns and war movies, McQueen's stature was solidified by such films as 'Love With the Proper Stranger' and 'Baby the Rain Must Fall': moody, modern romances that made the most of his bad-boy sex appeal. He earned his only Oscar nomination as a cynical sailor in 'The Sand Pebbles' (1966) and showed a surprisingly suave side as the millionaire bank robber in 'The Thomas Crown Affair' (1968). But whether in uniform or a three-piece suit, he was always the coiled, cool loner whose steely gaze and spontaneous grin barely hinted at the smoldering emotions underneath. (Photograph by William Claxton) —Michael Sauter

ESSENTIAL GIBSON

THE ROAD WARRIOR
(1981) As a post-nuke Man With No Name in the galvanizing actioner, Gibson made U.S. audiences take notice.

THE YEAR OF LIVING DANGEROUSLY
(1983) Showing that he had the right romantic-idol stuff as an amoral reporter in Peter Weir's swooning historical drama.

LETHAL WEAPON
(1987) As Danny Glover's suicidal partner, he broke through plastic Hollywood plotting with daft and dangerous sexiness.

HAMLET
(1990) They all laughed when Mel announced his intention to play the melancholy Dane—but the result was a fine and thoughtful Hollywood Hamlet.

BRAVEHEART
(1995) His second outing as a director gained him an Oscar for his rousing yet appropriately brutal tale of Scottish rebel William Wallace.

ESSENTIAL HESTON

THE TEN COMMANDMENTS
(1956) Letting his people go—right down the middle of the Red Sea—as a towering Moses in the DeMille classic.

TOUCH OF EVIL
(1958) He's a flummoxed figure of rectitude trying to plumb border corruption in Welles' masterful film noir.

BEN-HUR
(1959) Who would you want driving your chariot? Heston won an Oscar as a proud slave in ancient Rome in this massive epic.

EL CID
(1961) Another historical superhero: an 11th-century Spanish patriot driving the Moors back to Africa.

PLANET OF THE APES
(1968) He serves as a flawed stand-in for mankind stranded in a simian society in the classic sci-fi drama.

Heston

Charlton

Heston

"He's got these great blue eyes that take you in but erect a barrier and push you away" **LINDA HUNT** on Gibson

FROM THE MOMENT he stepped onto the screen as the postapocalyptic drifter in 1981's 'Mad Max' sequel, 'The Road Warrior,' Gibson exuded a peculiarly deranged charm. His image—hair disheveled, face smeared with soot, blue eyes wild (and, of course, the obligatory weaponry)—signaled a disruptive presence amid formula fare: Here was the truly unhinged action hero.

The vast popularity of the 'Mad Max' and 'Lethal Weapon' trilogies blunted Gibson's wackiness into a shtick, but audiences loved him. He won male admirers with his zany grit—and female fans with his magnetism—in films like 1983's 'The Year of Living Dangerously' and 1988's 'Tequila Sunrise.' He could even direct: After the modest success of 1993's 'The Man Without a Face,' he scored big at the box office—and won the Best Director Oscar—for 1995's Scottish epic 'Braveheart.'

But it's when Gibson starts blowing away bad guys that his star muscles truly flex. Using big guns and fast quips to delineate his own warped screen presence, he has established a persona larger than any individual picture—and turned even mindless fun into something rather more unsettling. (Photograph by Peggy Sirota)—Nisid Hajari

HESTON'S SCREEN PERSONA may now seem as outdated as the epics in which he starred—too large, too assured, too noble to be believed. (It's telling that Heston bookended his 50-year career by posing nude for art students to make ends meet—his statuesque body was seen as a '40s ideal—and by mocking himself in ironic '90s Bud Lite commercials.) In the 1950s, however, that steel-jawed rectitude defined Hollywood heroism, and Heston could plausibly inhabit roles as towering as Michelangelo, Moses, John the Baptist, and, later, even God. Our age may no longer trust such colossal figures, but with those fervent turns Heston established himself as the kind of larger-than-life figure we rarely see on screen today. (Photograph by Bill Avery)—NH

Mel
Gibson

Bruce Willis

IT MAY NOT be fashionable to say so, but the guy just might turn out to be our next Bogart. In fact, if you look at his entire filmography, Willis has consistently alternated big-budget behemoths (all those 'Die Hard's) with small-scale portraiture (1989's 'In Country,' 1994's 'Nobody's Fool')—movies in which his cockiness gets riddled with bleak doubt. For a while, his hey-I'm-a-star smugness was hard to swallow, but maybe 'Hudson Hawk' and 'The Last Boy Scout' (both 1991) were things he needed to work out of his system. Lately, with his bamboozled boxer in 'Pulp Fiction' and weary time traveler in '12 Monkeys,' the two sides of Willis' persona appear to be merging. He will not age gracefully. We can't wait. —TB

"He's very confident. He has a real sense of self, and he doesn't apologize for who he is or what he has." DEMI MOORE

"I'VE MADE a career," Kirk Douglas once said, "of playing sons of bitches." Indeed, the former Issur Danielovitch was an actor who could grab moviegoers by their lapels and lift them right out of their seats. Though his first few roles were as softies, he found the SOB within playing boxer Midge Kelly in 'Champion' (1949). That won him an Oscar nod, as did performances as the ruthless producer in 'The Bad and the Beautiful' (1952) and as an anguished Vincent van Gogh in 'Lust for Life' (1956). Whoever he was—Doc Holliday, Spartacus—Douglas would demand our attention. In a way, he was always the champion pleading, "I don't want to be a 'Hey, you!' all my life. I want people to call me 'Mister.'" (Photograph by Sharland) —Steve Wulf

Kirk Douglas

ESSENTIAL FLYNN

CAPTAIN BLOOD
(1935) The greatest pirate movie ever? Certainly the one that debuted all the great clichés of the genre—and made Flynn a star.

THE ADVENTURES OF ROBIN HOOD
(1938) You can keep Kevin Costner—Flynn's high-flying Robin of Locksley still has unbeatable panache.

THE DAWN PATROL
(1938) Proving he could act as well as buckle swashes in a fine, tough-minded WWI flying drama.

THEY DIED WITH THEIR BOOTS ON
(1941) A charismatic comic-book Custer in a history lesson as only Hollywood made 'em.

GENTLEMAN JIM
(1942) At the peak of his powers as boxer Jim Corbett in a raffish, bare-knuckled tale of 19th-century San Francisco.

ESSENTIAL STALLONE

ROCKY
(1976) On screen and off, it was the kind of fairy tale that movies always promise and real life hardly ever delivers.

NIGHTHAWKS
(1981) The best of his early action roles, as a New York City SWAT-team ace facing off against Rutger Hauer in a tram high above the East River.

FIRST BLOOD
(1982) He first played John Rambo, morally gutted Vietnam vet, in this tough, well-made, and, yes, thoughtful, action pic.

RAMBO: FIRST BLOOD PART II
(1985) A less complex, more gung-ho Rambo—and just in time for the zeitgeist. A huge hit, it sums up Reagan-era pop culture for better and worse.

CLIFFHANGER
(1993) The best of his latter-day action roles, as a mountain climber forced to hit the peaks by gold-hungry terrorists.

Sylvester
Stallone

THE PHENOMENAL SUCCESS of the 'Rocky' movies had already draped the proper myth around Stallone's cartoonishly muscular frame. So when John Rambo strapped on his overstuffed bandolier in 1985's 'Rambo: First Blood Part II' and single-handedly refought the Vietnam War—while, in the same year, Rocky KO'd Russian superman Ivan Drago in 'Rocky IV'—Stallone locked into the decade's pulse like a neutron bomb. Since then, he has looked less sly as the tides of macho have retreated around him: He has tried comedy, drama, sci-fi—everything but Beckett, it seems. The turning point of his career is near. Off screen, the man possesses a beguiling sense of irony, and it would be a pity if he didn't find a way to let it finally bleed onto film. Rimbaud II, anyone? (Photograph by Neil Leifer) —TB

"He was a bit of a sadistic devil, was Errol, but it was done with such charm and sense of mischief that he was always forgiven." **STEWART GRANGER**

AS BEFITTING the archetypal Robin Hood, Errol Flynn robbed from his own life to give to others. Even before this handsome devil from Tasmania became a screen idol, he was a sailor, gold hunter, slave trader, and journalist. After his starring role in 'Captain Blood' (1935), Flynn became Hollywood's swashiest buckler, portraying such heroes—real and imagined—as Robin of Locksley, Gentleman Jim Corbett, and Don Juan. He played them so convincingly because he was them. The end of his own picture, though, was sadly hastened by scandal, drink, and drugs, and he died in 1959 at age 50. In 'They Died With Their Boots On' (1941), Flynn—as General Custer—is asked where he's going, and he replies, "To hell or glory. It depends upon your point of view."—SW

Errol
Flynn

Douglas Fairbanks Sr

HE WAS THE FIRST action hero. As Zorro, D'Artagnan, and the Thief of Baghdad, Fairbanks thrilled audiences with his derring-do: shimmying up trees, bounding from one galloping horse to another, hurling himself from rampart to castle wall. Like America itself in the 1920s, Fairbanks was feverishly energetic, fatally optimistic, and hell-bent on risk. And, for a time, he was Hollywood's most famous star. When he and bride Mary Pickford moved into their Hollywood estate, Pickfair, the couple became, as Alistair Cooke once wrote, "living proof of America's chronic belief in happy endings"— no matter that they eventually split or that his career faded. He will always be remembered for winning the fight, the girl, and the glory. —David Hochman

"IF ARNOLD hadn't existed," said 'Conan' director John Milius, "we would have had to build him." In truth, Schwarzenegger built himself: Born and raised in Austria, he has morphed Andrew Carnegie's self-made man with Charles Atlas' self-made he-man. That he went from a Hollywood joke to the physical embodiment of Reagan-era America (the more powerfully so as that era faded into history) is a tribute to Schwarzenegger's genuine, witty, and rarely acknowledged poise.

It was as a dim Teutonic bodybuilder that he washed up on these shores in the late '60s, winning a raft of Mr. Universe titles even as Hollywood kicked sand in his face. It took the success of 'The Terminator' (1984) on video and pay cable to prove that Arnold was onto himself as a goof. "Ah'll be beck," he said in that movie, and he was, in a series of action films that escalated the mayhem and gradually widened his appeal. He moved into comedy (in 1988's 'Twins') with the adroitness of a mergers-and-acquisitions ace, and his marriage to Kennedy kid Maria Shriver made the immigrant saga complete. Schwarzenegger now bestrides modern Hollywood like a grinning, rippled Colossus of Rhodes— the meeting of man and special effects. He will never do Shakespeare. You may hate all that he stands for. He couldn't care less. (Photograph by Andrew Eccles) —TB

Arnold Schwarzenegger

ESSENTIAL SCHWARZENEGGER

PUMPING IRON
(1977) A wry documentary on the bodybuilding subculture that let Arnold show his natural charisma by playing himself.

THE TERMINATOR
(1984) The film that let it be known that Arnold was in on the joke—still one of the most influential action movies of recent years.

TOTAL RECALL
(1990) A blissfully cynical sci-fi thriller, this asked us to believe that, even brainwashed, he could be a family man. We did.

TERMINATOR 2: JUDGMENT DAY
(1991) The special effects almost stole the show in the epic sequel—until Arnold strode on as a now-decent cyborg.

JUNIOR
(1994) The best of his periodic attempts at outright comedy, playing a pregnant man with a beguilingly straight face.

ESSENTIAL FAIRBANKS

THE MARK OF ZORRO
(1920) Fairbanks first found his swashbuckling rhythm—after 31 films—in this high-spirited adventure classic.

THE THREE MUSKÉTEERS
(1921) A long-cherished desire to play D'Artagnan finally comes true, with much snappy swordplay.

THE THIEF OF BAGDAD
(1924) Amid the astonishing Arabian nights sets, he stands out as a grinning, lightning-fast, carpet-riding hero.

THE BLACK PIRATE
(1926) Fairbanks takes to the high seas for this improbable but salty tale of a good guy gone colorfully bad.

THE TAMING OF THE SHREW
(1929) Fairbanks and wife Mary Pickford's first film together—and a talkie, yet—cast the duo as Shakespeare's battling lovers.

The Rebels

FOR ALL OF ITS catering to our hopes and fantasies, Hollywood has always been a deeply conservative company town, with rules of propriety all the more rigid for never having been written down. There are those who have broken the rules and paid horribly: Frances Farmer, John Garfield, Fatty Arbuckle. And there are those who have turned it to their advantage by giving the flouting of convention a whole new allure. Hollywood despises failed rebels, but it adores, mimics—and eventually absorbs—the successful ones.

Take Ingrid Bergman, damned on the floor of the Senate in 1950 as an immoral wench for ditching husband Petter Lindstrom in favor of director Roberto Rossellini and welcomed back, with crocodile tears and an Oscar (for 'Anastasia'), a mere six years later. Granted, heterosexual straying was easier to forgive then; being gay was accepted within the industry only if you played the game. Poor Monty Clift never seemed to decide what camp he was in—all he had going for him was raw talent and the face of an agonized angel—and that uncertainty lit up his films while muting his career.

With the rise of youth culture, the demise of the studio system, and the martyrdom of Saint James Dean, the Hollywood rebel became just another brilliant subtype. Jack Nicholson, Jane Fonda, Susan Sarandon—all would have been crushed like bugs if Louis B. Mayer or Harry Cohn were still running the show. And in the '90s, we have come to expect our matinee idols to spit epithets and punch out photographers. Perhaps a new breed of rebel—thoughtful, polite, wearing a necktie—is just around the corner. —Ty Burr

James Dean's portrayal of teen angst in 1955's 'Rebel Without a Cause' heralded the rise of a youth culture that hastened the fall of the studio system—and made the rebel a Hollywood staple

"I WAS INFORMED you were the most beautiful woman ever to visit Casablanca," Claude Rains tells her in 1942's 'Casablanca.' "That is a gross understatement." Indeed, there are many who say Bergman was the most beautiful woman ever to visit Hollywood. David O. Selznick brought her there from Stockholm after seeing her in the Swedish version of 'Intermezzo.' (He remade it in English, with Bergman again playing the concert pianist in love with a married violinist.) Bergman had a noble and natural beauty, a charming lilt, a world of talent—and a little bit of luck. She supplanted Hedy Lamarr in 'Casablanca' and Irene Dunne in 'Gaslight,' which won her 1944's Best Actress Oscar. She could play good women ('The Bells of St. Mary's'), bad women ('Saratoga Trunk'), and both ('Notorious'). But when Bergman's life began to imitate her art—she left her family for director Roberto Rossellini in 1949—America gave her the scarlet 'A,' and she fled to Europe. Fortunately for us, she returned in 1956's 'Anastasia' and won her second Oscar. She scored a third, as Best Supporting Actress, for 'Murder on the Orient Express' (1974). "I've gone from saint to whore and back to saint again, all in one lifetime," she once said. The symmetry went even further. In her last great movie role, 'Autumn Sonata' (1978), she played a concert pianist. (Photograph by Gordon Parks) —Steve Wulf

Ingrid
Bergman

"He was a very brilliant actor and a luminous young man. I can still see him, learning to play Bach on his recorder, looking like an angel on earth." **JULIE HARRIS**

James Dean

WHAT NOWADAYS would take a dowel through the nose or an amplifier turned up to 11, James Dean could provide with a furrow of his brow. The too-brief record he left after his untimely death at age 24 (only three films in two years) openly signals the volcanic disenchantment that went into their making: One critic compared his performance in 'Rebel Without a Cause' (1955) to that of a savage marveling at a mirror, while another likened leaving the theater after 'East of Eden' that same year to exiting a loony bin. Today, Dean's passion hasn't dimmed because he spoke less for a generation than for the timeless wisdom that smoldered beneath his raging antics. (Photograph by Dennis Stock) —Nisid Hajari

SHE MAY ALWAYS feel the heat for her offscreen fervor, but whether crusading against the Vietnam War or exhorting devotees to new aerobic heights, Fonda easily matched that intensity in her best on-screen work. Being Henry's daughter wasn't as big a ticket to Hollywood as her doe-eyed sexiness; it carried her through her early career and several luscious roles in films by first husband Roger Vadim (like 1967's 'Barbarella'). But the fiercely bleak spirits she evoked in movies like 'They Shoot Horses, Don't They?' (1969) and 'Klute' (1971)—for which she won her first Oscar—confirmed her as a performer with range and determination, as open to risk in her acting as in her often unpopular public stands. It is in these roles, with eyes fiery and uncompromising, that viewers truly feel the burn. (Photograph by Peter Basch) —NH

WHENEVER YOU FEAR she's about to become the earnest Eleanor Roosevelt of Hollywood—whenever the nation cringes as she and live-in love Tim Robbins approach the Oscar podium—Sarandon rights all with the unvarnished clarity of her acting. It's tough to believe that the woman behind Marmee of 1994's 'Little Women' or Sister Helen of 1995's 'Dead Man Walking' once played hippie chicks (1970's 'Joe') or campy squares (1975's 'Rocky Horror Picture Show') or a succession of vivid, thinking man's sex bombs (1980's 'Atlantic City,' 1988's 'Bull Durham,' 1990's 'White Palace')—until you see 'Thelma & Louise,' in which all the parts of Sarandon's on-screen personae come together with a harrowing yet satisfying kaboom. (Photograph by Timothy White) —TB

"She has the energy and strength of a thousand women"
JULIA ROBERTS on Sarandon

Susan
Sarandon

Barbra
Streisand

"Any entrepreneur who believes he has another Barbra Streisand tucked away on a pedestal, waiting to be unveiled, had better change professions. There is not going to be another Barbra Streisand, now or ever." ALAN JAY LERNER

FITTINGLY, HE CARRIED a photo of Franz Kafka with him wherever he went. Clift was a brooding, Kafkaesque soul—alcoholic, confused about his sexuality, and reluctant to embrace fame. It was only through his friendships (with Liz Taylor and others) and his work that he found strength (particularly after a 1957 car wreck left his flawless face disfigured). Exorcising his personal demons on screen made Clift Hollywood's first darkside-of-the-moon actor (paving the way for everyone from Marlon Brando to Jennifer Jason Leigh). Clift's angst electrified movies such as 'Red River' (1948), 'A Place in the Sun' (1951), and 'From Here to Eternity' (1953), but it also made mincemeat of him. Asked once how he'd sum up his life, Clift said, "I've been knifed." (Photograph by Burt Glinn)   David Hochman

SHE WAS THE ugly duckling who willed herself into a swan. With her unconventional looks and Brooklyn bluster, Streisand seemed an improbable star, but as a singer, she could wrench emotion from the unlikeliest tunes. She translated this flair for the dramatic to the screen, where she won an Oscar her first time out for the 1968 musical 'Funny Girl.' When she fought for control in Hollywood—commandeering 'A Star Is Born' (1976), championing 'Yentl' (1983)—her reputation as a perfectionist megalomaniac seemed to overshadow her extraordinary gifts. But like many of the heroines she's played—the hooker defending her sanity in 'Nuts' (1987), the passionate shrink in 'The Prince of Tides' (1991)—Streisand has emerged from the struggle as stubborn, as provocative, and as compelling as ever. (Photograph by Steve Schapiro) —N H

Montgomery
Clift

Peter O'Toole

PLAYING HEROES wounded more by doubt and self-mockery than by anything the bad guys could dish out, O'Toole was an Errol Flynn for the age of neurosis. He burst like a blue-eyed supernova upon the scene in 'Lawrence of Arabia' (1962); as Noël Coward told him, "If you had been any prettier, it would have been Florence of Arabia." With 'Becket' (1964) and 'The Lion in Winter' (1968), O'Toole painted himself into a period-film corner, and for years he seemed lost to brawls and booze. But he came back with a battered magnificence as a godlike director in 'The Stunt Man' (1980) and turned potential self-parody into a series of lovely grace notes in 'My Favorite Year' (1982)—for which he earned his seventh Oscar nod. (Photograph by Bob Willoughby) —TB

"You couldn't take your eyes off him on screen. He looked like a beautiful, emaciated secretary bird.... His voice had a crack like a whip." RICHARD BURTON, on O'Toole

NICHOLSON IS AN on-screen Puck for the generation that came of age in the '60s. To his credit, he knows this. He has made it the subject of his best performances. 'Five Easy Pieces' (1970) asks if such a creature has responsibilities toward other people, 'Carnal Knowledge' (1971) wonders where sexual charisma shades into misogyny, and 'One Flew Over the Cuckoo's Nest' (1975) shows the price society exacts for acting the renegade fool. And when Nicholson plays it close to the chest, as in 'Chinatown' (1974), he conveys a riveting exhaustion—the truculence of the earthbound sprite.

That all those performances came in the early 1970s says less about how Nicholson has changed than it does about Hollywood. He is more popular than ever, winning Oscars (for 1983's 'Terms of Endearment') and beloved as the last uncompromised antihero of the wacky '60s. But it's a mark of our age's inability to come to terms with Jack that he is cast ever more frequently as monsters ('Witches of Eastwick,' 'Batman'). Still, his mad glint keeps our hopes burning, and does anyone doubt that he will once again find flesh in which to sink those killer teeth? (Photograph by Peggy Sirota) —TB

Jack Nicholson

IN THE STRIVING, backbiting scramble that is the movie business, there are a lucky few for whom gossip stops once the camera starts rolling. They have the respect and admiration of their peers. Their presence on a marquee is a guarantor for audiences seeking particular pleasures. These are the pros: players who take their gifts to such heights, or whose approach to movie acting is so consistent, that they are to the average star what T-bills are to junk bonds. You can bank on them.

They have all the attributes of other celebrities except visible neurosis; in its place is an enjoyment of, if not an obsession with, craft. There may be no star as lost in his metronomic métier as Fred Astaire; the reason he needs

Pros

Ginger is to remind himself that others are there at all. Lon Chaney set himself the task of meticulously burying body and face under layers of grotesquerie—and then relocating the human being beneath. Stanwyck defines the Hollywood trouper, Gene Kelly the athletic hoofer. Joan Crawford—well, yes, she was vain, but in film after film after film she made vanity her subject, and survival was the subtext of her characters and career.

It's hard to recognize the pros of today, perhaps because movie stars make fewer films. Both Jodie Foster and Anthony Hopkins, though, have been around long enough, and applied themselves to enough movies both glorious and thankless, to be honored with laurels here. If neither is the type of star to incite passion in audiences, our response nevertheless falls somewhere on the scale between affection and awe. And thankfulness, for setting the standards of quality so high for everyone else. —Ty Burr

1925's Phantom
may well be his most
ous characterization,
t Chaney approached
is roles with singular
centration. Tirelessly
experimenting with
makeup, lighting, and
movement, he was the
consummate pro.

SHE'S BETTER KNOWN now as Mommie Dearest, but it was Saint Joan of the teary eyes and rigid mouth who ruled women's weepies in the Golden Age. A creature of sheer will, Crawford was a flapper in the '20s, a coutured tootsie in the '30s, an abused romantic in the '40s, a campy spectacle in the '50s—and both a horror-movie star and a Pepsi board member in the '60s. 'Mildred Pierce' (1945) won her an Oscar—and revenge on theater owners who had once called her "box office poison." But see the swooning 'Humoresque' (1946) or the nutty 'Johnny Guitar' (1954) if you want to catch her determination in all its neurotic glory. (Photograph by Clarence Sinclair Bull) —TB

"The nearer the camera, the more tender and yielding she became. The camera saw, I suspect, a side of her that no flesh-and-blood lover ever saw."
GEORGE CUKOR

Joan
rawford

ESSENTIAL CRAWFORD

DANCING LADY
(1933) A typically breezy
romp with Clark Gable,
her constant costar and
sometime lover in
the early days.

MILDRED PIERCE
(1945) She righted a
faltering career and won an
Oscar as the put-upon
heroine of a grand
kitchen-sink melodrama.

HUMORESQUE
(1946) One of the very best
Hollywood weepies, a
lush confection in which
married Crawford fiddles
with violinist John Garfield.

JOHNNY GUITAR
(1954) Nicholas Ray had
a high time directing this
bonkers-but-fascinating
psycho-feminist Western.
It's doubtful the star was
in on the joke.

**WHAT EVER HAPPENED
TO BABY JANE?**
(1962, above) She
couldn't have missed the
macabre wit in this one,
but undoubtedly took
comfort in the fact that her
character, Blanche, had been
a bigger movie star than
sister Jane (Bette Davis).

IT'S AMAZING what an appetite for fava beans, Chianti, and human flesh can do for a career. Hopkins was long regarded as a capable and occasionally even brilliant actor. But after 27 minutes of screen time as Hannibal Lecter in 1991's 'The Silence of the Lambs'—for which he won a Best Actor Oscar—Hopkins became a supernova. Ever since, he's given a series of devastating performances, including his Oscar-nominated roles in 'The Remains of the Day' (1993) and 'Nixon' (1995). Of the latter, he said, "I'm just trying to play the human being." That is the core of his greatness—finding the souls in men seemingly without them. (Photograph by Nigel Parry) —David Hochman

Anthony
Hopkins

"I've directed a lot of great actors, but Tony's simply the best. He'll risk everything for you. Every time."
OLIVER STONE

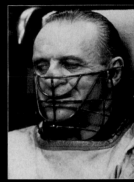

ESSENTIAL FOSTER

TAXI DRIVER
(1976) Effortlessly showing both sides of a child prostitute: the angel of Travis Bickle's rescue fantasies and the raw, messed-up kid.

THE LITTLE GIRL WHO LIVES DOWN THE LANE
(1976) A brainy little chiller that pits a kid with bodies in her basement against a very skanky Martin Sheen.

THE ACCUSED
(1988) Foster's unsentimental performance as a gang-rape victim brought her a deserved Best Actress Oscar.

FIVE CORNERS
(1988) A neighborhood slice o' life that works magic via a loopy script from John Patrick Shanley ('Moonstruck') and Foster's easy authority.

THE SILENCE OF THE LAMBS
(1991) A second Oscar, as the novice fed tracking a serial killer and coming up hard against evil Anthony Hopkins.

ESSENTIAL STANWYCK

STELLA DALLAS
(1937) Without Stanwyck's canny toughness as a lower-class mom who gives up her daughter, this classic would dissolve in sugar.

REMEMBER THE NIGHT
(1940) Another one of director Mitchell Leisen's peerlessly sexy romances, with the star a shoplifter warmed by prosecutor Fred MacMurray.

BALL OF FIRE
(1941) She's an on-the-lam tootsy who teaches professor Gary Cooper about linguistics and love. Maybe her best comedy performance.

THE LADY EVE
(1941) Or maybe it's this one, as a con man's shady daughter who falls for rich boob Henry Fonda.

DOUBLE INDEMNITY
(1944) A cheap blond viper, luring sap MacMurray into sex and murder in a thriller that's imitated to this day.

Jodie Foster

FOSTER IS AT an interesting crossroads now—as if any moment in a life spent before the camera were not interesting. Just shy of 35, she has already won two Best Actress Oscars (for 1988's 'The Accused' and 1991's 'The Silence of the Lambs') and proved her worth as a director (with 1991's 'Little Man Tate'). That she survived a career as a child actor apparently psychically intact is even more impressive, especially given some of the films into which the spookily capable Foster found her way ('Taxi Driver,' 'The Little Girl Who Lives Down the Lane'). She has rarely bothered with conventional romantic leads, although when she stoops to it, as in the underrated 'Sommersby' (1993) or the rollicking 'Maverick' (1994), she can play with the best.

What is left for her to conquer? Even Foster seems unsure at the moment. 1994's 'Nell' was a backwoods love triangle as ungainly as its heroine's vowels; her second turn behind the camera, 1995's 'Home for the Holidays,' was a self-indulgent Thanksgiving turkey. Yet it is doubtful that any actress who has made watchful common sense seem so glamorous will ever be the subject of an article titled "Can This Career Be Saved?" Like her predecessor in levelheaded allure, Katharine Hepburn, Foster does not really seem to need movie stardom—and that is a power to make the hardiest of Hollywood players tremble. (Photograph by Firooz Zahedi) —TB

"If God had designed
a perfect acting
machine, it would be
pretty close to Jodie."
JON AMIEL, director

A LOT OF ACTRESSES played dames in the movies, but with Stanwyck you felt as if she'd really done time behind the diner counter. A onetime Follies girl named Ruby Stevens, she grew into a thoroughgoing professional adored by the directors and largely male crews with whom she worked (Herman Mankiewicz had a memorable fantasy about being married to her and coming home to find her waiting with an apple pie she had baked herself—and no panties). She was a cynical delight in screwball comedies like 'The Lady Eve' (1941), a touching working-class heroine of melodramas like 'Stella Dallas' (1937), and a cynosure of peroxided bourgeois evil as the Venus flytrap of 'Double Indemnity' (1944). (Photograph by John Engstead) —TB

Barbara Stanwyck

Lon Chaney

HE WAS THE GREATEST special effect in silent movies and, before his early death from bronchial cancer in 1930, had finally made the transition to sound with the hit 'The Unholy Three.' No actor ever morphed himself with such cruel imagination: For 'The Hunchback of Notre Dame' (1923), Chaney harnessed 20 pounds of plaster to his back and underwent three hours of make-up; he bound his legs to play an amputee in 'The Penalty' (1920); in 'The Phantom of the Opera' (1925), he disfigured his nose by gluing it with fish skin. But the Man of a Thousand Faces wasn't just a primordial Freddy Kreuger. The reason his films last—why he is still the face of the Hunchback or the Phantom to people who have never even heard of Lon Chaney—is the raw human hurt evident in even his most monstrous of monsters. —TB

"Chaney carved for himself a niche in motion pictures so unique that it is doubtful it will ever again be filled. He was a sincere artist and a splendid gentleman."
CECIL B. DEMILLE

BORN IN A Brooklyn tenement, Hayward had the aggressive drive of a woman hell-bent on escaping squalor; that she found stardom playing alcoholics, a death-row inmate, and a ruthless rag-trade queen must have been a heavy irony. Hayward bounced around Hollywood in the late '40s, with only 1947's 'Smash-Up—The Story of a Woman' giving a hint of what was to come. 'I Can Get It for You Wholesale' (1951) propelled her to the front ranks, but it was in two nonfiction roles—as boozy actress Lillian Roth in 'I'll Cry Tomorrow' (1955) and condemned murderess Barbara Graham (for which she won a Best Actress Oscar) in 'I Want to Live!' (1958)—that Hayward found her métier as embattled tigress. —TB

Susan Hayward

SUSAN HAYWARD
in Paramount Pictures

P2553

Gene Kelly

PERHAPS THE BEST movie-musical segment of all time belongs to Gene Kelly: dancing and splashing in 'Singin' in the Rain' (1952), the Hollywood broadside he head-lined and codirected. A former dance instructor and gas-station attendant, Kelly did college theater and summer stock before starring in 'Pal Joey' on Broadway in 1940. From there, it was just a two-step to MGM. As a dancer, he was the thunder to Fred Astaire's lightning, and as a choreographer, he was a true genius. 'Anchors Aweigh' (1945) accounted for his only Oscar nomination, but it was just the start of his string of classics: 'On the Town' (1949), 'An American in Paris' (1951), 'Singin' in the Rain.'... What a glorious feeling Kelly brought to the screen. (Photograph by John Engstead) —Steve Wulf

"What do dancers think of Fred Astaire? It's no secret. We hate him. His perfection is an absurdity, and that's hard to face." MIKHAIL BARYSHNIKOV

Fred
staire

IT'S DIFFICULT TO believe that Astaire existed off screen: He seems like a celluloid phantom, a trick of the light. In truth, those gaspingly perfect dance routines were the product of endless, grueling practice. Astaire came up through vaudeville and Broadway with his sister, Adele, but when he hit Hollywood on his own, it was as a nimble art deco stick figure paired with the sassy exuberance of Ginger Rogers. Their films together—'Follow the Fleet' (1936), 'Carefree' (1938), and the rest—are wonderful, yet to watch Astaire dance alone is to witness movement bewitched by itself. He hid his art behind the artifice of top hat and tails. Look closely, though, and you'll see a working definition of grace. —TB

The End

ADDITIONAL CREDITS